18 Golden Steps to
Transform Your Life

Vinod Nair is a US Fulbright Scholar and alumnus of IIM Bangalore and Carnegie Mellon University. His career spans 28+ years of global leadership as a serial entrepreneur, venture builder, investor and mentor. He has had the privilege of building and scaling multiple businesses across diverse markets with clarity, integrity and purpose.

Guided by the spirit of the *18 Golden Steps*, Vinod strives to live a life rooted in discipline, humility and transformation. Deeply committed to bringing India's timeless wisdom into practical application, he offers this book with gratitude and sincerity, as a companion for seekers and professionals aspiring towards balance, strength and lasting transformation.

18 Golden Steps to Transform Your Life

A Practical Guide Inspired by Swamy Ayyappa

VINOD NAIR

RUPA

Published by
Rupa Publications India Pvt. Ltd 2026
7/16, Ansari Road, Daryaganj
New Delhi 110002

Sales centres:
Bengaluru Chennai
Hyderabad Jaipur Kathmandu
Kolkata Mumbai Prayagraj

P-ISBN: 978-93-5352-219-3
E-ISBN: 978-93-5352-652-8

First impression 2026

10 9 8 7 6 5 4 3 2 1

Printed in India

Dedication

To my beloved parents Leela Nair and VNB Nair, who taught me that true progress begins with quiet gratitude and steady effort. Your calm strength, gentle guidance and unwavering love have shaped my life far more deeply than I will ever be able to express.

I offer this book with deep gratitude for every sacrifice you made and every hope you held for me. May Swamy Ayyappa bless you both with a long, healthy and deeply satisfying life. May His grace surround your days with peace, His light guide your years and His protection keep you always in bliss.

This book is a small offering of thanks for the countless ways you helped me become more than I ever imagined.

Gratitude

Om Swamiye Sharanam Ayyappa

Before beginning this journey, I pause to bow in gratitude. All the wisdom, all the insights, and all the clarity that appear in these pages are gifts far greater than any human effort. Any goodness in these words belongs to the Divine—to Swamy Ayyappa, whose life and teachings illuminate the path for all who seek courage, compassion and clarity.

All mistakes, all lapses in expression, all missteps in understanding are mine alone. I accept full responsibility for them and offer them with humility at the feet of the source of all guidance.

This book is written with a heart full of thanks to the countless pilgrims, seekers, scholars and practitioners whose lives silently shape the living tradition of Sabarimala. Each story, each ritual, each insight is a thread woven into a tapestry far greater than the Self.

May anyone who reads these words find the courage to walk their own path with integrity, the patience to honour each step along the way, and the clarity to see the light within themselves and within all beings. May this book be a humble offering that sparks reflection, action and devotion.

All glory is to the Divine. All lessons are yours to receive. All shortcomings are mine to own.

This book is an offering of devotion. All proceeds from its sale are committed to Sabarimala in gratitude for the timeless tradition that continues to guide countless pilgrims.

Invocation

Om Swamiye Sharanam Ayyappa!

O Lord of the Sacred Hills, son of dharma and
embodiment of unity,
guide our steps as we walk the forest paths of life.
Let the fires of discipline burn away our ignorance,
let the river of compassion cleanse our hearts,
and let the 18 steps of wisdom lead us
to the sanctum where only You remain.
We bow to You, the One who accepts all,
the friend of the devotee,
the light in the darkness,
the silence in the noise,
the truth in all appearances.
O Lord of the Holy Hill, son of Hari and Hara,
Protector of dharma, embodiment of compassion and
discipline, we bow at Your lotus feet.
Grant us clarity to walk the path You have shown,
Strength to uphold truth,
And humility to see the Divine in all beings.
Lead us from the darkness of ignorance to the light of
self-realization,
From the bondage of ego to the freedom of moksha.

Om Swamiye Sharanam Ayyappa!

Contents

PATH OF THE PRACTICE

Bringing Ayyappa's Wisdom Home

Foreword

Sabarimala is more than a destination. It is a journey of the mind, a training for the senses and a celebration of equality that transcends caste, class and creed. From the very first step, the pilgrimage speaks a timeless truth: *Tat Tvam Asi*—'You are that.' The Divine you seek is not somewhere far away. It is already within your own innermost self, waiting to be recognized and lived!

Every ritual of Sabarimala, from wearing the sacred *mala* to carrying the *irumudi*, is designed to guide the pilgrim *inward*, to cultivate discipline, focus and self-awareness. Every social custom, from walking in unity to serving fellow pilgrims, directs attention *outward*, fostering humility, empathy and equality. Together, these inward and outward practices form a complete, living path that is perfectly suited for the challenges of modern life.

Sabarimala is not only a pilgrimage to a hilltop temple. It is a practice that trains the heart, strengthens the mind and empowers action. It reminds us that true strength is gentle, courage is patient and devotion is practical. For the youth of today, the lessons of Sabarimala are not relics of the past. They are tools to navigate a world of complexity, opportunity and ethical choices.

This book is your companion to carry the spirit of Sabarimala in your daily life. It shows you how the discipline of the steps, the mindfulness of the rituals and the clarity of Vedanta can be applied to study, work, relationships and personal growth. It is an invitation to live as a pilgrim every day, to see the Divine in yourself and in all beings, and to walk a path of courage, compassion and conscious action.

How to use this book

This book is meant to be your practical guide, your travel companion and your daily 'reflection partner'. Treat it not just as a text to read, but as a living tool to shape your life. Each chapter offers short practices, checklists, meditations and reflections designed to be immediately useful.

This book is structured in **two complementary paths** to guide your journey clearly:

PATH OF THE STEPS: 18 GOLDEN STEPS TO A BETTER LIFE

This section represents the 18 steps that every pilgrim climbs on the journey to Sabarimala. Each step is a symbol, a principle and a way of being that has the potential to transform your life. By understanding and reflecting on these steps, you gain timeless tools for personal growth, courage, discipline and inner strength.

PATH OF THE PRACTICE: BRINGING AYYAPPA'S WISDOM HOME

This section takes the wisdom of the 18 steps and shows you how to apply it in your everyday life. It contains practical tips, exercises, reflections and habit-building practices that help you integrate these teachings into work, study, relationships and personal growth. It is designed to be a companion for your transformation journey, helping you bridge the spiritual and the modern with ease and insight.

The language of this book is intentionally simple, allowing the depth of its teachings to be accessible without jargon. Its aim is to guide you towards reflection, action and transformation. Treat it as a companion that walks with you, offering guidance, insight and practical tools to navigate every challenge with courage, compassion and clarity.

Use it to pause, to reset, to act, to reflect and to grow. Let the practices become habits, let the reflections become insight and let the steps become your path. Each time you engage with this book, you are not just reading, you are walking, learning and aligning your life with the timeless wisdom of Swamy Ayyappa and the teachings of Vedanta.

Symbolism of the 18 Golden Steps

The sacred 18 golden steps of Sabarimala, revered as *Pathinettampadi*, are far more than a passage into the sanctum. They are a spiritual ascent, a divine ladder guiding every devotee from the bondage of the material world to the bliss of union with Lord Ayyappa. Each step is a gateway of transformation, demanding that the pilgrim shed layers of ego, desire and ignorance to attain purity and grace.

THE SYMBOLISM OF THE 18 STEPS

- ***Panchendriyas* (5 Senses):** The first five steps signify mastery over the senses of sight, hearing, smell, taste and touch, without which the mind remains restless and scattered.
- ***Ashtaragas* (8 Human Passions):** The next eight steps call upon the devotee to conquer the turbulent emotions and vices: *Kama* (desire), *Krodha* (anger), *Lobha* (greed), *Moha* (delusion), *Mada* (pride), *Matsarya* (jealousy), *Ahamkara* (ego) and *Asuya* (envy). Only by transcending these does the heart become fit for devotion.

- ***Trigunas* (3 Fundamental Qualities):** The next three steps represent the cosmic forces of *Satva* (purity and harmony), *Rajas* (passion and activity) and *Tamas* (ignorance and inertia). The devotee must rise above their imbalance to attain inner equilibrium.
- ***Vidya and Avidya* (Knowledge and Ignorance):** The final two steps embody the eternal choice between light and darkness, wisdom and delusion, truth and falsehood. Crossing them is the soul's triumph over ignorance, entering into the radiance of true knowledge.

The Ascent: To ascend the Pathinettampadi is to enact the highest spiritual journey, a surrender of the lower self and an awakening into divine consciousness. Only when the senses are stilled, the passions subdued, the *guna*s transcended and ignorance dispelled, does the pilgrim become worthy to stand before Lord Ayyappa and receive His infinite blessings.

PATH OF THE STEPS

18 Golden Steps to a Better Life

The Sacred Power of 18

In Hindu thought, numbers are never mere quantities. They are vibrations of truth, carriers of meaning and doorways into deeper understanding. Among them, the number 18 shines with extraordinary significance. Across scripture, philosophy and sacred practice, 18 emerges repeatedly as a symbol of completeness, struggle, transformation and the final victory of *dharma*.

18 IN THE SCRIPTURES

The *Mahabharata,* the vast ocean of dharma, is woven into 18 *parva*s (books). The Kurukshetra war itself was fought for 18 days, not by accident but by cosmic design. Those 18 days mirror the inner war that every seeker must wage, a battle not only against outer forces but also against the illusions within. The *Bhagavad Gita,* born on that battlefield, carries its immortal wisdom in 18 chapters. Besides the *Mahabharata,* there are 18 *Purana*s, 18 *Upapurana*s and 18 *Dharma Shastra*s (*Smriti*s).

18 IN VEDANTA AND PHILOSOPHY

Vedanta speaks of 18 elements that constitute the human experience: the senses, the organs of action, the mind, intellect and the subtle forces that bind us to the material world. To cross beyond these is to awaken to the Self that is timeless and free. In this way, 18 becomes a threshold number. It marks the passage from bondage to release, from entanglement in *prakriti* to union with *purusha*, the eternal spirit.

18 IN PILGRIMAGE AND SABARIMALA

This sacred symbolism comes alive most vividly at Sabarimala. Every pilgrim knows that to reach the sanctum of Lord Ayyappa, one must climb the 18 golden steps, the *Pathinettampadi*. These are not simply stones placed in sequence. They are symbols of the journey within: five senses to master, eight passions to subdue, three *guna*s to harmonize, and finally, the embrace of knowledge as ignorance falls away. To place one's foot on each step is to declare, 'I am rising above what holds me down. I am climbing towards my Lord.'

THE COSMIC RHYTHM OF 18

Why does 18 echo so often across scripture and ritual? Because it reflects an eternal truth that spiritual progress is not haphazard, it is ordered. The path is not chaos, it is rhythm. The number 18 embodies wholeness, struggle, balance and transcendence. It is the union of opposites, the alignment of knowledge and action, surrender and effort, human striving and divine grace.

FROM THE SACRED NUMBER TO THE GOLDEN STEPS

In this book, we will not only reflect on the mystery of 18 but also walk it as a living process. The 18 golden steps of Sabarimala are not only for the temple hill; they are thresholds of the soul. Here, we will use the allegory of the sacred steps to lay out a practical path: 18 steps to transform your life. Each step is a discipline, a practice and a promise. Together, they form a staircase that can carry you from the ordinary to the extraordinary, from distraction to focus, from restlessness to realization.

So, as pilgrims climb the hill to see Ayyappa, this book invites you to climb the inner hill within yourself. The number 18 is no longer just a symbol; it becomes your roadmap. These 18 golden steps are offered as a way to live with courage, clarity, humility and devotion. And, at the summit of that climb, as on the mountain of Sabarimala itself, awaits not only *darshan* of the Lord but the discovery of your highest Self.

The Mountain Path to the Self

The story of Sabarimala is not just about a temple atop a hill in Kerala. It is about a journey that is both outward and inward. It is a journey that transforms the pilgrim into a seeker, the seeker into a devotee and the devotee into one who has had a glimpse of the eternal truth.

For centuries, the shrine of Lord Ayyappa has drawn millions from across India and beyond. What is remarkable is not just the scale of devotion, but the fact that here, in the dense forests of the Western Ghats, social differences melt away. Men and women, rich and poor, literate and illiterate, upper caste and lower caste, Hindu, Muslim and Christian, all become *Swamy* or *Malikappuram* in the eyes of each other. No one is higher or lower, for in the gaze of Ayyappa all are equal.

Yet the pilgrimage is not easy. The physical journey to Sabarimala is demanding, but it is the **41-day *vrata*,** the period of discipline and purification, that truly shapes the devotee. It demands control of the senses, detachment from comforts and a constant remembrance of the Divine

The heart of this journey are the **18 golden steps**

(Pathinettampadi) that lead to the sanctum sanctorum. Each step is symbolic. Each is a stage of inner transformation. When the devotee climbs them, it is not merely the body that ascends, but the soul that draws nearer to the Supreme.

In this book, we will use the allegory of the sacred 18 steps as a framework for an 18-step process to transform one's life. We will connect the wisdom of Ayyappa's life and teachings with the timeless truths of Vedanta especially the great declaration *Tat Tvam Asi*. We will see how these truths are not only relevant in the ancient world, but they are also vital for the modern youth navigating the complexity of the twenty-first century.

The aim is not to turn this into a mere historical or religious manual, but a **living guide,** a companion you can turn to daily, just as the pilgrim turns to his mala (rosary) each day of the vrata. By walking these 18 steps in your life, you walk towards the Divine within.

So, let us set foot on the very first step and walk the path of the Lord, through the lessons of discipline, towards the final realization of oneness with the Divine. **The mountain path awaits.**

GOLDEN STEP ONE
Renunciation

When a devotee begins the pilgrimage to Sabarimala, the first thing he learns is that this is not a casual trip to a hill temple. The journey begins long before the forest path, long before the climb, and even, long before the irumudi *kettu* is tied across the shoulders. It begins with a decision in the heart, the decision to renounce.

Renunciation in the path of Ayyappa does not mean abandoning life or escaping responsibility. It means a conscious choice to loosen the grip of attachment to pleasures, comforts and the ego's endless demands. The vrata that precedes the pilgrimage is rooted in this principle. For 41 days, the devotee commits to a life of simplicity, celibacy, vegetarianism, humility and constant remembrance of the Lord.

THE CALL TO LET GO

The moment you wear the mala, you symbolically set down

the baggage of your worldly identity. In that moment, your name changes. You are no longer simply a person with a job, a family and social titles. You are now Swamy. This is not a title of superiority, but of surrender. To call each other Swamy is to acknowledge that each one is a servant of the Divine, and at the same time, a manifestation of the Divine.

This act of renunciation is subtle yet profound. In the modern world, we are encouraged to build and cling to identities. We are told to hold tight to our achievements, our possessions, and our status. But the first step towards Ayyappa is the opposite, letting go of all these outer layers so that the inner truth can be seen.

THE EXAMPLE OF AYYAPPA

In the life of Swamy Ayyappa, renunciation appears repeatedly. Born of the union of Vishnu (in the form of Mohini) and Shiva, He was destined for greatness. Yet as the prince of Pandalam, He showed no interest in ruling for personal gain. His focus was always on protecting dharma, serving the people and fulfilling His divine mission.

When the kingdom celebrated His victories over injustice, Ayyappa did not cling to glory. When the time came for Him to leave the palace and take His place in the forest shrine, He did so without hesitation, renouncing royal comforts. His example teaches us that true strength lies not in what we hold on to, but in what we can willingly let go of.

THE VEDANTIC CONNECTION

In Vedanta, the Self that we usually identify with the body, the mind, the ego is seen as temporary. The real Self, the *Atman,* is eternal and untouched by worldly gain or loss. To realize this Self, one must loosen attachment to the unreal. This is called *vairagya,* dispassion towards the transient.

Renunciation in Ayyappa's path is a training in vairagya. It is not suppression or self-punishment, but a gradual turning of the mind towards what truly matters. By saying 'no' to certain habits and indulgences during the vrata, the devotee is actually saying 'yes' to the possibility of deeper joy.

RELEVANCE FOR MODERN LIFE

To today's youth, renunciation might seem like a distant or outdated concept. But in truth, it is more relevant than ever. The modern world bombards us with distractions. We live in an age where attention is a commodity and where our desires are constantly stimulated by advertising, social media and peer pressure.

Renunciation here does not have to mean abandoning all pleasures forever. It means learning to master our desires instead of being mastered by them. It means being able to put aside the phone for an hour to meditate, to resist the urge to respond to every impulse and to choose depth over constant stimulation.

The vrata of Ayyappa is a perfect training ground for this skill. In those 41 days, you prove to yourself that you are capable of discipline, that you can live without certain comforts and that your happiness does not depend on instant gratification.

THE INNER WORK

When you begin the first step, the renunciation, you may notice the mind reacting. It will complain about discomfort, it will justify breaking small rules, it will try to negotiate with your resolve. This is the nature of the ego when faced with change. But in staying firm, you begin to observe the mind instead of being controlled by it.

Every time you say no to a temptation during the vrata, you are taking another step towards inner freedom. You begin to understand what the ancient sages meant when they said that the real bondage is not the chains outside, but the chains we put on ourselves through craving and aversion.

DAILY PRACTICE FOR STEP ONE

- **Morning Reflection:** On waking, touch the mala and say, 'I am not this body, I am not this mind, I am the servant of the Lord.'
- **Simplicity Check:** Before you eat, ask yourself, 'Am I eating to nourish the body or to please the tongue?' Choose what nourishes.
- **Digital Renunciation:** Dedicate at least one hour a day without any screen or device. Use that time for prayer, chanting or silent reflection.
- **Identity Reminder:** Address others as Swamy or Malikappuram in your heart, even if you are not on the pilgrimage. This practice breaks the habit of judging others by status or role.

CLOSING THOUGHT

The first golden step is not just a ritual; it is the foundation for everything that follows. Without renunciation, the mind remains restless, scattered and unable to receive the higher truths. With renunciation, even in small doses, the mind begins to clear, like a pond settling after the wind stops. **Ayyappa's first lesson is simple yet transformative: you cannot climb the mountain while carrying the weight of your attachments. Put them down and you will find your climb becoming easier.**

GOLDEN STEP TWO
Control of the Senses

Once the devotee has committed to renunciation, the next step on the path to Sabarimala is to master the senses. If renunciation is about loosening attachment to possessions and status, sense control is about guiding the five gates of perception so they serve the soul rather than enslave it.

The human senses are gifts. They allow us to taste, smell, touch, see and hear the world. But they can also be restless wanderers, constantly chasing pleasure and avoiding discomfort. In spiritual practice, unrestrained senses can scatter the mind and pull it away from the higher goal. Step two is about reclaiming mastery over these powerful forces.

WHY SENSE CONTROL MATTERS

Imagine a chariot pulled by five strong horses, each representing one of the senses. If the reins are loose, each horse will pull in a different direction, and the chariot will spin in confusion or crash. But if the charioteer holds the reins firmly, all the horses move in harmony towards the destination.

In the same way, your senses can either lead you towards clarity and inner peace or they can drag you into distraction, desire and dissatisfaction. The vrata of Swamy Ayyappa trains the devotee to become the charioteer.

LESSONS FROM AYYAPPA'S LIFE

Swamy Ayyappa's life is full of examples of sense control. Even as a child, He was trained in martial arts, scriptures and royal duties. These disciplines required Him to stay alert, focused, and balanced in body and mind. Despite being surrounded by palace luxuries, He remained detached and impervious to temptation.

One of the most telling moments comes from His confrontation with the demoness Mahishi. She tried to unsettle and overpower Him, but His mind was not disturbed. His victory was not only one of physical strength but also of complete mastery over fear, anger and distraction.

This mastery is what the devotee is asked to cultivate. By controlling the senses, you gain the power to choose your response to life instead of reacting impulsively.

THE VEDANTIC PERSPECTIVE

In Vedanta, the senses are compared to restless horses because they are naturally drawn outward. The mind follows them, and the intellect, if not vigilant, is swept away. The *Bhagavad Gita* teaches that sense control is not about suppressing experience but about redirecting it.

When the eyes see beauty, it can be an occasion for gratitude to the Creator rather than desire for possession. When the tongue tastes food, it can be an act of offering rather than indulgence. Sense control in this sense is transformation, not repression.

THE PRACTICE DURING THE VRATA

The 41-day preparation for Sabarimala includes many disciplines that develop sense control:

- **Dietary Discipline:** Eating only *sattvic* food, often cooked at home, avoiding meat, alcohol and overly spicy dishes.
- **Speech Discipline:** Avoiding gossip, harsh words and unnecessary chatter.
- **Visual Discipline:** Reducing entertainment that excites the senses or disturbs the mind.
- **Listening Discipline:** Choosing devotional music, mantras and silence over noise and distraction.
- **Touch Discipline:** Practising celibacy and respecting the sacredness of physical contact.

Over time, these practices sharpen awareness. You begin to notice how the senses pull you, and you learn to gently guide them back.

RELEVANCE FOR MODERN YOUTH

In the modern world, sensory overstimulation is constant. Notifications, advertisements, loud environments, fast food and binge-worthy entertainment are all designed to grab attention and keep it hooked. This creates a restless mind that finds stillness almost impossible.

Sense control today is not about rejecting modern life. It is about setting boundaries so the senses do not exhaust your inner energy. Turning off your phone for a set period each day, choosing mindful eating over rushed meals and listening deeply to someone without distraction are all acts of modern sense control.

When you gain mastery over your senses, you gain mastery over your life. You no longer chase every impulse. You choose where your energy goes.

THE SUBTLE BENEFITS

Sense control does not just bring peace; it brings power. When your senses are aligned, your mind becomes concentrated. Concentration leads to deeper meditation, and deeper meditation opens the door to spiritual insight.

On a practical level, sense control sharpens focus, improves memory and builds emotional resilience. You become less reactive to provocation, less swayed by trends and more grounded in your own values.

DAILY PRACTICE FOR STEP TWO

- **Mindful Eating:** Eat in silence for at least one meal a day. Focus fully on the taste, texture and nourishment of each bite.
- **Silent Hour:** Keep one hour daily for silence, without

phone, television or conversation. Observe how the mind and senses behave.

- **Gratitude for Senses:** Each morning, offer thanks for one sense and use it to connect with the Divine. For example, listen to a mantra and dedicate that sense of hearing to Ayyappa.
- **Guarded Input:** Choose consciously what you read, watch and listen to. Ask yourself, 'Will this purify my mind or agitate it?'

CLOSING THOUGHT

Control of the senses is not a rejection of life's beauty; it is the refinement of it. Just as a musician tunes an instrument before playing, the devotee tunes the senses so they produce harmony rather than noise. **The second golden step reminds us that mastery begins within. If you can guide your senses, you can guide your destiny. And as you climb towards Ayyappa, each step of control becomes a step into freedom.**

GOLDEN STEP THREE
Purity of Mind

Purity of mind is the foundation of all spiritual progress. Without it, even renunciation and sense control will feel like hollow exercises. A mind that is pure is like a clear lake. It reflects truth without distortion. A mind that is impure is like muddy water. No matter how beautiful the surroundings, the reflection will be clouded.

When the devotee reaches the third golden step, the emphasis shifts from the external disciplines of lifestyle and sensory control to the subtler inner realm. This is where the pilgrimage becomes deeply transformative because the battle is no longer with what is outside but with what is within.

UNDERSTANDING PURITY OF MIND

Purity of mind does not mean emptiness of thought. It means freedom from thoughts that are harmful, selfish or binding. An impure mind is filled with jealousy, greed, resentment and pride. A pure mind is filled with compassion, contentment, humility and love for all beings.

The mind is constantly taking impressions from the senses, from memory and from imagination. Each impression leaves a trace, shaping the way we think and feel. Purity of mind is about cleansing these impressions and refusing to feed the ones that darken our awareness.

LESSONS FROM AYYAPPA'S LIFE

Swamy Ayyappa's life shows this purity in action. Even as a prince, He treated everyone equally, from courtiers to servants. His decisions were guided by fairness, not personal gain. When He faced challenges, His mind remained free from hatred towards His opponents. His actions were not driven by revenge but by the duty to protect and uplift.

One of the most striking qualities in the legends of Ayyappa is His ability to see beyond the surface. Where others saw enemies, He saw souls caught in ignorance. Where others saw threats, He saw opportunities to uphold dharma. This clarity comes only when the mind is free from the fog of selfish motives.

THE VEDANTIC PERSPECTIVE

In Vedanta, the mind is compared to a mirror. The soul, or Atman, is always pure, but the mind can become dusty with impressions and desires. Meditation, selfless service and righteous living act like a cloth that wipes away the dust, allowing the light of the Self to shine through.

The Upanishadic teaching of *Tat Tvam Asi* rests on this

purity. Without a pure mind, the truth of this statement cannot be realized. The impurities of ego and ignorance block the recognition of one's divine nature.

PURITY DURING THE VRATA

The disciplines of the 41-day vrata are designed to support mental purity:

- **Avoiding Arguments and Anger:** Devotees are encouraged to practise patience and speak gently.
- **Truthfulness:** No lying, exaggerating or misleading others.
- **Non-harming:** Not just physically, but in words and thoughts.
- **Avoidance of Lustful Thoughts:** Maintaining mental celibacy, not just physical restraint.

In addition, devotees engage in daily prayers, chanting of the Ayyappa Swamy mantra and reading of sacred texts. These practices occupy the mind with uplifting impressions, leaving little room for negativity to take root.

RELEVANCE FOR MODERN YOUTH

In today's world, the mind is under constant pressure. Social media feeds can fill it with envy, comparison and restlessness. News cycles can fill it with fear and anger. The workplace can fill it with stress and competition. All of these are impurities in the spiritual sense, because they cloud the natural joy of the soul.

Purity of mind, today, requires conscious curation of

mental input. It means choosing what to watch, read and think about with the same care one would choose clean food or pure water. It also means actively generating positive states of mind through gratitude, forgiveness and kindness.

THE SUBTLE BENEFITS

When the mind is pure, life feels lighter. Situations that once caused agitation lose their grip. You become less reactive and more reflective. Relationships improve because you approach others without suspicion or judgment. Creativity flows more freely because it is no longer blocked by anxiety or resentment.

A pure mind is also more receptive to spiritual insight. Meditation deepens, and the connection to the Divine becomes natural and effortless.

DAILY PRACTICE FOR STEP THREE

- **Morning Intention:** Begin the day by setting the intention to keep your mind free from harmful thoughts.
- **Mental Diet:** Just as you avoid unhealthy food, avoid mental inputs that feed anger, greed or fear.
- **Forgiveness Practice:** Each evening, think of anyone you feel resentment towards, and consciously release it.
- **Gratitude List:** Write down three things each day that you are thankful for. Gratitude is one of the fastest purifiers of the mind.

CLOSING THOUGHT

The third golden step reminds us that the mind is the real temple. You can travel to the holiest of places, but if your mind is filled with impurity, you will not see the sanctity around you. Purity of mind turns every place into Sabarimala because it allows you to see the Divine everywhere. **When the mind is pure, the path to God is clear. When it is impure, the path is blocked by illusions of the ego. The third golden step is the clearing of that path, making space for the light of Ayyappa to guide the way.**

GOLDEN STEP FOUR
Truthfulness

Truthfulness is the jewel among virtues. Without it, no relationship can survive, no trust can grow and no spiritual path can bear fruit. The fourth golden step at Sabarimala calls the devotee to live in perfect alignment with truth in thought, word and action.

Truthfulness is not only about avoiding lies. It is about living in such a way that your life itself is a statement of truth. It means being genuine, transparent and consistent with your inner values. When your actions match your words and your words match your inner convictions, you walk in truth.

THE DIVINE EXAMPLE OF AYYAPPA

The life of Swamy Ayyappa is marked by unwavering truthfulness. He never deceived, even when telling the truth brought personal risk. In the legends, when confronted with difficult situations, He did not hide behind half-truths or clever wordplay. His clarity of speech reflected the purity of His heart.

One story tells of how Ayyappa, as a young prince, was given the task of obtaining tiger's milk to heal His foster mother's mysterious illness. This request was part of a plot against Him, yet Ayyappa accepted it without deception or complaint. He trusted that truth and dharma would guide the outcome. His honesty in action inspired faith in all who heard of His journey.

THE VEDANTIC UNDERSTANDING OF TRUTH

In Vedanta, truth is not just a moral guideline. It is the nature of reality itself. The Sanskrit word for truth, *satya,* comes from *sat,* meaning 'being' or 'existence'. To live in truth is to live in harmony with the ultimate reality. When the *Chandogya Upanishad* declares *Satyam Eva Jayate,* i.e. truth alone triumphs, it is stating that truth is indestructible because it is aligned with the eternal.

Falsehood, on the other hand, is a distortion of reality. It creates layers of illusion that block the light of the Self. Even small lies can weigh heavily on the mind, creating fear of exposure and breaking the flow of peace.

TRUTHFULNESS IN THE 41-DAY VRATA

During the 41-day vrata, truthfulness is practised with precision. Devotees are expected to:

- Speak only what is true and beneficial.
- Avoid gossip and criticism.

- Keep promises and commitments, no matter how small.
- Confess mistakes rather than cover them up.

Truthfulness also extends to self-reflection. A devotee must be honest with himself about his motives, strengths and weaknesses. Without this self-honesty, other spiritual disciplines lose their depth.

TRUTH IN MODERN LIFE

In today's world, truth often competes with convenience. People lie to avoid conflict, to protect their image or to gain advantage. Advertising sometimes bends facts to sell products. Social media can present curated versions of reality that are far from the truth.

For the modern youth, truthfulness is both a challenge and a liberation. Choosing truth may require courage, especially when it is unpopular. Yet it also brings great relief, because you no longer need to maintain a facade. You can be at ease with yourself, knowing you have nothing to hide.

SPEAKING THE TRUTH WITH COMPASSION

Truth is powerful, but like fire, it must be handled with care. Harsh truth can wound, while compassionate truth can heal. A devotee of Ayyappa learns to speak the truth in a way that uplifts rather than destroys. This is the balance between satya (truth) and *ahimsa* (non-harming).

Ayyappa himself embodied this balance. His words were direct but never cruel. He could correct wrongdoing without humiliating the wrongdoer. This is the art of truthful communication.

THE INNER TRUTH

Beyond factual accuracy lies the deeper truth of self-realization. This truth is not about external events but about who you are at the core. The highest truth of Vedanta is that you are not the body or the mind, but the eternal, unchanging Self. Realizing this truth is the goal of all spiritual practice.

When you live in harmony with this inner truth, fear fades away. Lies are born of fear—fear of loss, fear of judgment, fear of failure. When you know your essence is beyond harm, you have no reason to lie.

DAILY PRACTICE FOR STEP FOUR

- **Morning Affirmation:** Begin the day with the statement, 'I will live in truth today in thought, word and deed.'
- **Truth Check:** Before speaking, ask yourself, 'Is it true? Is it necessary? Is it kind?'
- **End-of-day Review:** Reflect on any moment you compromised the truth, and decide how to correct it.
- **Silent Practice:** Spend a few minutes each day in silence, listening for the truth that arises from within when the noise of the mind settles.

CLOSING THOUGHT

The fourth golden step is a call to live in full transparency with life itself. Truthfulness aligns you with the very structure of reality. It clears the fog of deception, allowing you to walk with steady steps towards God. When truth fills your life, you become fearless, because you stand on the unshakable ground of reality. **You become like Ayyappa, whose words were as steady as his heart, whose life was a living embodiment of truth.**

GOLDEN STEP FIVE
Compassion

Compassion is the fragrance of the heart when it blossoms in love for all beings. It is the ability to feel the joys and sorrows of others as if they were your own. The fifth golden step at Sabarimala reminds the devotee that spiritual growth is meaningless without kindness and empathy.

Compassion is not mere sentiment. It is a force that moves you to act for the well-being of others, even when it requires sacrifice. In Sanskrit, this quality is called *karuna*, and it is counted among the highest virtues in the yogic and Vedantic traditions.

THE COMPASSION OF SWAMY AYYAPPA

Swamy Ayyappa's life is a story woven with acts of compassion. Despite being a warrior and protector, His heart was tender towards those in need. The most famous example is His friendship with Vavar, a Muslim warrior.

Instead of treating Vavar as an enemy, Ayyappa recognized his strength and goodness. Their mutual respect grew into a deep friendship, which is honoured at Sabarimala to this day through the presence of the Vavar mosque near the temple.

In another tale, Ayyappa healed those afflicted by disease, protected the vulnerable from wild animals and ensured that justice was tempered with mercy. His compassion crossed the boundaries of religion, caste and social position.

THE VEDANTIC ROOTS OF COMPASSION

Vedanta teaches that all beings share the same Self. When you truly see the divine essence in others, compassion arises naturally. The recognition of oneness makes cruelty impossible. To harm another is to harm yourself, and to help another is to serve God directly.

The great sages of India did not limit compassion to humans alone. They extended it to animals, plants and even the Earth itself. This universal compassion reflects the understanding that all of existence is woven from the same divine fabric.

COMPASSION IN THE 41-DAY VRATA

During the 41-day vrata, devotees are encouraged to express compassion in practical ways:

- Offering food to the hungry without expectation of reward.
- Helping fellow devotees in their journey, especially those who are older or weaker.

- Forgiving those who may have wronged you.
- Caring for animals and avoiding harm to any living being.

The vrata is not only a personal discipline but a training ground for selfless service. The physical austerities prepare the mind, but it is compassion that opens the heart.

COMPASSION IN THE MODERN WORLD

Today, the pace of life and constant competition can make compassion seem like a luxury. People are often too absorbed in their own struggles to notice the needs of others. Yet the modern world, with its divisions and conflicts, is in desperate need of compassionate action.

For the youth, compassion is a power that can transform relationships, workplaces and communities. Simple acts, like listening without judgment or offering encouragement, can have profound ripple effects. Compassion is not weakness; it requires courage to care in a world that can sometimes feel indifferent.

THE DISCIPLINE OF ACTIVE KINDNESS

True compassion is not passive. It does not stop at feeling sorry for someone. It moves into action. The devotee learns to ask, 'What can I do right now to ease this suffering?' Sometimes the answer is material help, sometimes it is emotional support and sometimes it is simply being present with another person in their pain.

Ayyappa's example shows that compassion can coexist

with strength. Being compassionate does not mean ignoring wrongdoing; it means addressing it with the aim of restoring balance and harmony, not simply punishing.

COMPASSION AS A PATH TO GOD

In the Bhakti tradition, love and compassion are considered direct paths to God. A heart softened by compassion becomes a fit vessel for divine grace. As the *Bhagavata Purana* says, 'Where compassion flows, God resides.'

Compassion also has the power to dissolve the ego. When your focus shifts from 'What can I get?' to 'What can I give?', the walls of selfishness begin to crumble. This brings you closer to the state of selflessness that is essential for union with the Divine.

DAILY PRACTICE FOR STEP FIVE

- **Morning Offering:** Begin the day by mentally offering your words, thoughts and actions for the good of all beings.
- **Compassion Pause:** When faced with conflict, take a moment to consider the other person's perspective.
- **Act of Service:** Each day, perform at least one act of kindness without telling anyone.
- **Expand Your Circle:** Include not just friends but strangers and even those you dislike in your prayers and good wishes.

CLOSING THOUGHT

The fifth golden step is a reminder that the heart must be as strong in love as the body is in discipline. Compassion is the bridge that connects the soul to the soul of another. It dissolves the barriers of religion, caste and status, revealing the shared light within. To walk this step is to walk with Ayyappa's own heart, seeing the world not through the eyes of judgment but through the eyes of love.

GOLDEN STEP SIX
Humility

Humility is the quiet strength that allows you to stand tall without standing over others. It is the understanding that all beings share the same divine essence, no matter their position, education or wealth. In the eyes of Lord Ayyappa, the king and the commoner, the scholar and the labourer, the rich and the poor are all Swamys walking the same path. On the pilgrimage, this truth is lived every day. You eat from the same vessel as others, sleep in the same open space, and walk barefoot on the same rough road. No one's worth is measured by their bank balance, job title or fame.

Humility is not weakness. It is the wisdom of knowing that the source of your talents and opportunities is beyond you. It allows you to use your gifts in service rather than in self-display. It enables you to lift others without needing to stand higher yourself.

HOW IT WORKS ON THE PILGRIM PATH

On the Sabarimala journey, every pilgrim is called Swamy. This is not just a polite title. It is a reminder that the same divinity resides in all. The wealthy pilgrim might serve food to the poor pilgrim. The elder might receive guidance from the young. The experienced might walk at the pace of the beginner. Service is valued more than recognition.

This step protects the heart from pride when things go well and from shame when things go wrong. It teaches you to serve with sincerity whether or not anyone notices, and to accept praise with the understanding that you are only a channel for the Divine.

HOW THIS APPLIES IN MODERN LIFE

Humility is as powerful in the workplace and the home as it is on the pilgrimage path. It helps you learn faster because you are willing to listen to others. It builds trust because people feel respected in your presence. It deepens relationships because you are not always trying to win or prove yourself right.

In leadership, humility means you take responsibility when things go wrong and share the credit when things go right. In family life, it means valuing each person's contribution, no matter how small. In personal growth, it means staying open to learning from anyone, regardless of their background or position.

EXAMPLES IN MODERN LIFE

- A manager gives public credit to their team while quietly working extra hours to ensure success.

- A teacher learns a new method from a student without feeling insulted.
- A skilled professional takes time to thank the support staff whose unseen work makes their success possible.

Humility softens the ego so that wisdom, cooperation and compassion can flow more freely.

DAILY PRACTICE FOR STEP SIX

- **Morning Reflection:** Begin your day by remembering that everyone you meet carries the same divine spark you do. Before stepping out, say silently, 'May I see the Swamy in all today.'
- **Equal Greeting:** Greet each person you meet, from the doorman to the director, with the same warmth and respect. Let your eyes, tone and body language reflect equality.
- **Gratitude before Credit:** When you receive praise, pause and acknowledge silently all the people, resources and blessings that helped make it possible. Offer a small prayer of thanks before responding.
- **Anonymous Service:** Once a week, perform an act of kindness that no one can trace back to you. Let the joy of service be its own reward.
- **Night Review:** Before sleep, think of one moment in the day when you let go of pride and acted with humility. Thank Ayyappa for that grace, and ask for more of it tomorrow.

A PILGRIM'S STORY

A pilgrim from a large city once joined a group from a small village for the 41-day vrata and the climb. In his daily life, he was used to people standing when he entered the room. On the path to Sabarimala, no one cared about his position. One evening, while serving food to fellow Swamys, he noticed an elderly man struggling to carry water. Without hesitation, he took the heavy pot and walked with him to the shelter. Later he discovered that the man was a simple farmer. Yet in that moment, the pilgrim felt he was serving Ayyappa Himself. He returned home with a changed heart, treating the office janitor with the same respect as the board chairman.

CLOSING THOUGHT

The sixth golden step is the step that keeps every other step steady. Without it, renunciation can become pride in sacrifice, truth can become a weapon and devotion can become a display. With it, every action becomes worship. When you see all beings as equal, you walk the Earth more lightly, and the Divine walks more clearly through you.

To live this step is to live as a true pilgrim every day. Whether you are in a temple, a market, an office or a home, humility will keep your heart open, your service pure and your path straight. As you climb the 18 golden steps, let humility be the quiet music beneath your feet, carrying you closer to the One who bows to none yet bows to all.

GOLDEN STEP SEVEN
Patience

Patience is the art of trusting the process without forcing the pace. It is the calm strength that allows you to accept delays, endure discomfort and wait for the right moment without frustration. On the path to Sabarimala, patience is not simply a virtue; it is a necessity. The journey is long, the rituals are many and the discipline requires time to bear fruit. Without patience, the mind becomes restless, the body becomes weary and the heart loses its focus.

Patience is not passive. It is an active choice to remain steady in thought and action while trusting that the Divine has a perfect timing for everything. It is saying, 'I will do my part with full sincerity, and I will leave the results to Ayyappa.'

HOW IT WORKS ON THE PILGRIM PATH

From the moment a pilgrim begins the 41-day vrata, patience becomes his silent companion. The daily discipline can feel repetitive. The walk to the temple is slow and often uncomfortable. There are moments when the crowd is overwhelming and progress seems impossible. Yet the pilgrim knows that every step, however small, is part of the journey.

On the climb to the holy 18 steps, no one rushes ahead to finish first. Each step is taken with devotion, each pause filled with prayer. The temple itself is reached not through haste but through steady, mindful movement.

Patience also shows in how pilgrims treat each other. A slower walker is not pushed aside but supported. A tired pilgrim is encouraged to rest and then continue. The journey becomes a lesson in slowing down and honouring the pace of both body and spirit.

LESSONS FROM AYYAPPA'S LIFE

Ayyappa's life was a living example of patience. He did not resist the path the Divine had laid out for Him, even when it required long preparation and silent endurance. When tasked with bringing the milk of a tigress, He did not argue or despair. He waited for the right moment, trusted the unfolding of events, and acted without haste. This patient trust in divine timing made His strength unshakable.

His life shows that patience is not about inactivity but about allowing the right conditions to emerge before taking the next step.

HOW THIS APPLIES IN MODERN LIFE

In today's fast-moving world, patience often feels out of place. Technology gives us instant answers, businesses push for quick profits, and social media rewards immediate reactions. Yet the most valuable things in life still follow the ancient rhythm of slow growth. A meaningful relationship, a deep skill and a mature understanding of life all require patience.

In work, patience allows you to think strategically instead of chasing quick wins. In relationships, it helps you listen deeply and respond with empathy. In personal growth, it allows you to work through your weaknesses instead of becoming frustrated by them.

Patience in the modern world also means being able to wait for the right opportunity without becoming inactive. It is keeping your preparation steady so that when the moment comes, you are ready.

EXAMPLES IN MODERN LIFE

- A professional working towards a promotion focuses on building skills and relationships over several years rather than looking for shortcuts.
- A parent supports a child's learning pace instead of comparing them to others.
- A student accepts that mastery of a subject takes years of study and practice.

DAILY PRACTICE FOR STEP SEVEN

- **Morning Reflection:** Begin your day with the prayer, 'May I walk at the pace of the Divine today.' This sets the tone for a day of steady, unrushed action.
- **Mindful Waiting:** The next time you are in a queue or

stuck in traffic, use it as a moment to breathe deeply and repeat Ayyappa's name. Transform waiting into worship.

- **One Slow Activity:** Choose one task each day to do slowly and mindfully, whether it is drinking tea, writing an email, or walking to a meeting. This retrains the mind to value presence over speed.
- **Recognizing the Season:** Write down one area of your life where you are waiting for results. Reflect on what 'season' you are in. Is it a season for planting, growing or harvesting? This perspective makes waiting easier.
- **Night Review:** At the end of the day, recall one moment when you practised patience instead of rushing or reacting. Thank Ayyappa for giving you that moment of grace.

A PILGRIM'S STORY

A young pilgrim once became impatient on the steep climb to Sabarimala. The crowd was dense, the pace was slow and the heat was draining. He began to push ahead, determined to reach the temple quickly. An elder Swamy placed a hand on his shoulder and said, 'The temple will not move away. If you hurry, you will arrive in body but leave your mind behind. Walk with both together.' The young man slowed down. By the time he reached the sanctum, he understood that patience had allowed him to arrive not just at the temple, but within himself.

CLOSING THOUGHT

Patience is the steady flame that keeps the lamp of devotion burning. Without it, the fire of enthusiasm can quickly fade. With it, the journey becomes deeper and more meaningful. The climb to Sabarimala is not a race but a pilgrimage, and so is life.

When you practise patience, you move in harmony with the rhythm of the Divine. You allow blessings to ripen fully before receiving them. You see that waiting is not empty; it is filled with unseen preparation. **The seventh golden step invites you to trust that Ayyappa's timing is perfect, and that each moment of waiting is part of the sacred path.**

GOLDEN STEP EIGHT
Perseverance

Perseverance is the unwavering commitment to continue walking the path, no matter how steep the climb or how long the journey. It is the force that keeps the pilgrim moving even when the feet ache, the body tires and the mind whispers that it would be easier to give up.

The spiritual path is rarely a straight, smooth road. It has sharp turns, steep climbs and stretches where nothing seems to change. Perseverance means refusing to abandon the journey even in those stretches. It is the steady determination to keep showing up for your practices, duties and vows until the goal is reached.

Perseverance is not about speed. It is about constancy. Even if you move slowly, you still move forward. Like a lamp that burns through the night, perseverance allows devotion to keep glowing until the dawn.

HOW IT WORKS ON THE PILGRIM PATH

The 41-day vrata is a powerful training ground for perseverance. For some, the first days are filled with enthusiasm. But soon, challenges begin to appear: fatigue, discomfort, longing for familiar comforts or even doubts about whether the effort is worth it. Perseverance is what carries the devotee through these moments.

- When walking barefoot along rocky paths, perseverance says, 'One more step.'
- When hunger tempts you to break your fast, perseverance says, 'Stay the course.'
- When the early morning bath feels too cold, perseverance says, 'This discipline is part of my offering.'

It is not about never feeling discomfort or doubt, but about refusing to let those feelings decide your actions.

LESSONS FROM AYYAPPA'S LIFE

Ayyappa's mission to defeat Mahishi was not accomplished overnight. It required years of training, discipline and unshakable focus. He faced challenges that could have made Him turn back from dangerous enemies, harsh conditions and the weight of responsibility. Yet He pressed forward, step after step, without abandoning His purpose.

When His stepmother's false accusations sent Him into the forest, Ayyappa did not allow injustice to halt His journey. He accepted the challenge, prepared Himself and fulfilled the task with absolute commitment. His life shows that perseverance is the inner vow to never stop walking until the duty is done.

THE SPIRITUAL DIMENSION OF PERSEVERANCE

In spiritual practice, perseverance is the daily choice to continue even when there is no visible reward. Some days, prayer feels alive and full. Other days, it may feel dry or routine. The persevering devotee shows up in both conditions.

The fruits of spiritual discipline often ripen slowly. Perseverance is what ensures you are still present when they are ready to be received. It transforms temporary struggles into lasting strength.

PERSEVERANCE IN THE 41-DAY VRATA

For the Sabarimala pilgrim, perseverance is tested in many ways:

- The body adjusting to new routines and dietary restrictions.
- The mind resisting the loss of familiar comforts.
- The spirit facing the quiet inner challenges that arise in disciplined living.

Many start the vrata with energy but give up halfway because they expect instant transformation. Those who complete it understand that perseverance itself is the transformation. Every time you choose to continue despite discomfort, you strengthen not only your will but also your connection to Ayyappa.

LESSONS FROM NATURE

Nature gives us countless examples of perseverance. A river keeps flowing until it reaches the sea, never stopping because of a rock or a bend in its path. Roots push through the hardest soil to anchor a tree. Migrating birds travel thousands of miles each year, facing storms and exhaustion, yet they reach their destination.

Likewise, the devotee keeps walking towards the goal, no matter what obstacles appear. The road may change, the weather may shift, but the direction remains fixed.

PERSEVERANCE IN MODERN LIFE

In our times, distractions are constant. New goals compete for our attention and the temptation to quit when progress is slow is everywhere. Perseverance is what protects you from abandoning your purpose in the face of these pressures.

In work, perseverance means finishing what you begin even if recognition is delayed. In relationships, it means investing in understanding and care over many years. In self-development, it means showing up for your practice even when you do not feel like it.

EXAMPLES IN DAILY LIFE

- A student studying for a demanding exam who keeps revising after repeated failures.
- An entrepreneur facing multiple setbacks yet continuing to refine the vision.

- A volunteer serving a cause for years without seeking reward.

These modern forms of perseverance mirror the pilgrim's path—a commitment that does not depend on mood or ease.

DAILY PRACTICE FOR STEP EIGHT

- **Morning Resolve:** Begin the day with a clear statement: 'I will continue my path today, whatever comes.' This strengthens the mind to endure challenges.
- **One-more-step Approach:** When you feel like quitting a task, tell yourself to take one more step before deciding. Often, that step leads to renewed energy.
- **Track Your Consistency:** Mark a calendar for every day you complete your chosen discipline. Over time, the sight of steady progress becomes motivation in itself.
- **Find Strength in Example:** Read about saints, leaders or elders whose lives were marked by perseverance. Let their stories remind you that endurance is a sacred quality.
- **End-of-day Reflection:** At night, recall one moment when you wanted to stop but continued instead. Offer that moment to Ayyappa as an act of devotion.

A PILGRIM'S STORY

An elderly pilgrim once joined a group walking to Sabarimala. Midway, blisters formed on his feet and every step brought pain. His companions offered to arrange transport, but he refused. 'If my feet carry me only two steps a day, I will still reach the Lord's feet,' he said. He walked slowly, resting often, but never stopped. When he finally stood before the sanctum, his tears spoke of a joy earned through endurance.

CLOSING THOUGHT

Perseverance is the lifeblood of the pilgrim's journey. It does not seek the easiest way but the truest way. It does not stop when faced with difficulty but moves forward with quiet determination. This step reminds you that the sacred goal is reached not by bursts of speed, but by the unwavering steps of one who refuses to turn back. **The eighth golden step invites you to embody this spirit, to keep walking, to keep striving and to trust that every act of perseverance brings you closer to the divine embrace of Ayyappa.**

GOLDEN STEP NINE
Detachment from Materialism

The ninth golden step represents the art of living in the world without becoming bound by it. Detachment from materialism does not mean rejecting all possessions or living in poverty. It means enjoying and using what life provides without allowing it to control your happiness or define your identity.

AYYAPPA'S EXAMPLE OF DETACHMENT

Ayyappa was born as the divine son of Lord Shiva and Mohini, an incarnation of Lord Vishnu. Though destined for greatness, He lived with humility and simplicity. Even as a prince, He did not become attached to royal comforts. His heart was not fixed on palaces or wealth but on His duty and spiritual purpose.

When His mission on Earth was complete, He chose the forested hills of Sabarimala as His abode rather than any throne. This was not an escape from responsibility but a demonstration that true joy is found in the inner connection with the Divine, not in external possessions.

WHY DETACHMENT MATTERS IN SPIRITUAL LIFE

Material desires are endless. When one is fulfilled, another takes its place. If your sense of worth depends on what you own, you will live in constant anxiety over gaining and losing. Detachment brings peace because it removes the fear of loss.

Vedanta teaches that the world is transient. Houses crumble, wealth changes hands, and beauty fades. The only thing that remains is the eternal Self. When you recognize this, material objects lose their power over you.

THE ROLE OF DETACHMENT IN THE 41-DAY VRATA

During the pilgrimage vrata, devotees give up comforts and luxuries. They live with minimal clothing, simple food and no adornments. This is not about self-denial but about training the mind to find contentment in simplicity.

Walking barefoot on rough paths, sleeping on the floor and eating only what is offered helps the devotee see that happiness does not come from comfort. It comes from a quiet mind and a pure heart.

MODERN RELEVANCE

In today's consumer-driven world, people are often measured by their possessions. Advertisements constantly tell you that you need more to be happy. Detachment offers a different message: you are already complete.

This is especially important for young people. The race to have the newest phone, the latest fashion or the most followers online can lead to emptiness. Detachment teaches you to use things as tools, not as measures of your worth.

HOW TO PRACTISE DETACHMENT

- **Gratitude First:** Appreciate what you have without obsessing over what you do not have.
- **Use, Do Not Cling:** Enjoy possessions but be ready to part with them when necessary.
- **Buy Mindfully:** Ask yourself if you truly need something before purchasing.
- **Spend on Experiences:** Memories and learning stay with you longer than objects.

THE INNER JOY OF DETACHMENT

When you stop measuring life by possessions, you become free to enjoy the present moment. Detachment allows you to give more generously because you are not afraid of losing. It also makes you more resilient in times of change or loss.

Ayyappa's detachment did not make Him distant or cold. It made Him compassionate because He saw all beings as more important than things. His wealth was in wisdom and service.

CLOSING THOUGHT

The ninth golden step is the step of freedom from material bondage. By walking this step, you rise above the chase for more and learn to rest in the sufficiency of the present moment. Like Ayyappa, you can live fully in the world while keeping your heart anchored in the eternal.

GOLDEN STEP TEN
Gratitude

The tenth golden step calls the pilgrim to cultivate the sacred art of gratitude. Gratitude is not just a polite habit of saying 'thank you'. It is the recognition that life itself is a divine gift, that every breath, every opportunity, and even every challenge is woven into the tapestry of God's grace. This step teaches that gratitude is not a passing emotion, but a way of seeing the world, a constant awareness that the hand of the Divine is present in all moments.

AYYAPPA'S EXAMPLE OF GRATITUDE

In His earthly life, Ayyappa embodied gratitude through service, humility and devotion. He never considered His powers or achievements as His own. Every action was offered as an acknowledgment of the higher will guiding him.

One shining example is the story of the tiger's milk. Sent on a dangerous mission by His stepmother, Ayyappa could have seen it as an unjust demand. Yet He received it as an opportunity to serve and to fulfil His dharma. His heart was not burdened with resentment. Instead, He was grateful for the chance to act in alignment with the divine purpose. Gratitude transformed the task from a trial into a sacred offering.

For Ayyappa, gratitude was not reserved for times of victory or ease. It was present even in hardship. In the forest, during His long training, and in the solitude of penance, His heart remained thankful for the air that sustained Him, for the Earth that supported His feet, and for the unseen blessings that prepared Him for His mission.

THE POWER OF GRATITUDE

Gratitude has the power to transform how we experience life. Without it, even abundance can feel empty. With it, even scarcity can feel full. It changes the lens through which we see the world. Instead of asking, 'Why is this happening to me?' the grateful heart asks, 'What is this here to teach me?'

Modern psychology confirms what sages have taught for centuries: gratitude strengthens the mind, uplifts the spirit and even benefits physical health. But for the spiritual seeker, its importance goes beyond well-being. Gratitude aligns the heart with the Divine. It opens the channels through which grace flows freely into one's life.

GRATITUDE IN THE SPIRITUAL PATH

In the discipline of the 41-day vrata, gratitude is a constant companion. Each day, the devotee awakens early, bathes in cold water, eats simple food and walks barefoot, not as a hardship, but as a gift. Every meal is received with thanks. Every discomfort becomes an offering. Even the company of fellow pilgrims is recognized as a blessing, for they share in the sacred journey.

The path to Sabarimala itself becomes a living meditation on gratitude. The forests, rivers and hills are not just obstacles to cross, but reminders of the beauty and abundance of creation. A devotee who walks with gratitude finds joy in each step, knowing that the journey is as precious as the destination.

GRATITUDE IN MODERN LIFE

In today's fast-paced world, gratitude is often overshadowed by constant comparison and endless desire. Many measure their worth by what they lack rather than by what they have. This leads to a restless hunger that no possession or achievement can satisfy.

Gratitude offers a different path. It shifts focus from deficiency to abundance, from competition to appreciation. Whether you live in a bustling city or a quiet village, you can practise gratitude by noticing the blessings that already surround you—the support of family, the gift of health, the kindness of strangers, the chance to learn and grow.

Even in times of difficulty, gratitude softens the heart. A loss can be met with thanks for the time shared. A failure can be seen as a lesson in disguise. Gratitude does not deny pain, but it prevents pain from becoming bitterness.

DAILY PRACTICE FOR GRATITUDE

- **Morning Offering:** Begin each day by thanking the Divine for three blessings in your life, however small they may seem.
- **Gratitude Journal:** Write down moments each day when you felt thankful. Over time, this will train your mind to notice blessings more easily.
- **Verbal Acknowledgment:** Express thanks to people around you—family, friends, co-workers and even those who serve you in everyday life.
- **Mindful Pause:** When faced with difficulty, take a breath and silently say, 'Thank you for the lesson hidden here.'

THE INNER JOY OF GRATITUDE

When gratitude becomes a way of life, joy follows naturally. You no longer live in a constant state of wanting. Instead, you live in a state of receiving, not passively, but with a heart open to the gifts of each moment.

Gratitude also deepens relationships. A heart that recognizes and values the kindness of others draws more kindness towards it. Just as a garden thrives when watered, the bonds between people flourish when nurtured with appreciation.

AYYAPPA'S MESSAGE

Ayyappa's life teaches that gratitude is the foundation of spiritual wealth. Material possessions may come and go, but a grateful heart remains rich forever. He invites every devotee to see beyond the surface of events and recognize the hidden blessings that guide them closer to the Divine.

When you walk in gratitude, you walk in light. Every step becomes a prayer, every breath an offering, every challenge a gift in disguise.

CLOSING THOUGHT

The tenth golden step is the step of the thankful heart. Gratitude turns life into worship and worship into joy. When you choose to see the hand of the Divine in all things, you carry Ayyappa's light wherever you go. This light not only brightens your path but also warms the hearts of all who walk beside you.

GOLDEN STEP ELEVEN
Contentment

The eleventh golden step invites the pilgrim to discover the deep peace of contentment. Contentment is the ability to rest in the gift of life without the constant craving for more. It is the quiet strength that allows the heart to remain steady in both abundance and scarcity. True contentment is not laziness or resignation. It is the fruit of inner stability, born from the understanding that life is guided by a higher will and that the soul's needs are already met in the Divine.

AYYAPPA'S EXAMPLE OF CONTENTMENT

In His earthly journey, Ayyappa demonstrated contentment through His unwavering acceptance of the path given to Him. He did not demand comfort, recognition or reward. Whether in the royal palace or the solitude of the forest, His inner state remained the same. His sense of fulfilment came not from external circumstances, but from alignment with dharma.

During His years of learning and discipline, Ayyappa embraced a life of simplicity. He was content with what was provided, whether a humble meal or a resting place under the trees. Even when faced with challenges, His heart did not fall into complaint. His mission was clear, and His peace came from walking it without distraction. This unshakable balance became a source of strength for His devotees, showing them that true happiness is not tied to what one possesses, but to how one lives.

THE POWER OF CONTENTMENT

Contentment protects the mind from the endless cycle of desire. When one desire is met, another quickly takes its place. This restless chasing leaves little room for peace. Contentment, however, frees the heart from that race. It says, 'I have enough, I am enough, and this moment is enough.'

From a spiritual perspective, contentment is a sign of trust. It reflects the belief that what the Divine has given today is exactly what is needed for today. This does not mean one never works for improvement, but that the striving is no longer fuelled by dissatisfaction. Instead, it flows from a place of completeness.

CONTENTMENT IN VEDANTA

Vedanta teaches that the Self, the true essence of a person, is whole and unchanging. This wholeness does not depend on possessions, status or achievements. The one who realizes this truth lives with natural contentment, for nothing can add to or subtract from the Self.

When anchored in this understanding, a person is no longer tossed about by life's highs and lows. Joy does not swell uncontrollably when fortune rises, nor does sorrow drown the heart when fortune falls. The mind becomes like a calm lake, reflecting life as it is without distortion.

This state does not come from neglecting responsibilities or avoiding effort. On the contrary, one works with greater clarity and steadiness when no longer driven by the pressure of constant wanting.

CONTENTMENT IN THE 41-DAY VRATA

The discipline of the 41-day vrata is a living lesson in contentment. Devotees give up luxuries, sleep on the floor, eat simple vegetarian meals and walk long distances. In this simplicity, they discover that joy does not require abundance.

The pilgrim learns to be satisfied with the day's offering whether it is a handful of rice, a place in the shade, or the company of fellow seekers. Walking through forests, bathing in rivers, and sleeping beneath the stars awaken a deep appreciation for the natural provisions of the world. The heart begins to rest in the truth that very little is needed for a life of peace.

MODERN RELEVANCE

In today's world, contentment is often mistaken for complacency. The prevailing belief is that happiness comes only by achieving more, owning more, and becoming more. This constant pressure creates stress, anxiety, and a feeling that life is always lacking something.

Contentment offers a different way of living. It breaks the chain of comparison and teaches that value is not measured against others. A contented person is free from the exhausting need to prove worth through possessions or titles. This freedom brings not only inner peace, but also the ability to enjoy success without fear of losing it.

For young people growing up in a competitive and fast-changing world, contentment can be a shield against mental strain. It helps them focus on what truly matters—relationships, integrity, purpose—rather than chasing every fleeting trend.

HOW TO PRACTISE CONTENTMENT

- **Simplify Possessions:** Live with what you need and cherish it, rather than always reaching for the next new thing.
- **Limit Comparisons:** Remind yourself that your journey is unique, and measuring it against others is unfair to your own growth.
- **Pause before Desire:** When you want something, ask yourself whether it is essential or it is simply a passing craving.
- **Practise Acceptance:** Welcome the present moment as it is, without wishing it were different.

THE INNER JOY OF CONTENTMENT

When the heart rests in contentment, joy flows naturally. There is no need to wait for the perfect moment or condition to be happy. Life becomes a series of gifts, each one complete in itself. Even challenges lose some of their sharpness because the contented mind knows they, too, are part of the unfolding plan.

Contentment also strengthens relationships. When you are not looking to others to satisfy your wants constantly, you can appreciate them as they are. You stop seeing people through the lens of expectation and begin to see them through the lens of acceptance.

AYYAPPA'S MESSAGE

Ayyappa's life reminds us that contentment is a choice. It is the decision to anchor happiness within rather than in the changing tides of the world. This choice gives a strength that neither loss nor gain can shake.

The contented pilgrim walks with quiet dignity. Every step is steady, every breath unhurried, and every encounter received with grace. Such a pilgrim carries a peace that blesses not only themselves, but also those who cross their path.

CLOSING THOUGHT

The eleventh golden step is the step of the restful heart. Contentment frees the mind from the chains of endless desire and opens the way to lasting peace. In choosing contentment, you walk in harmony with the divine will, just as Ayyappa did. Your life becomes a testimony that joy is not found in having more, but in being fully present to what already is.

GOLDEN STEP TWELVE
Devotion to the Guru

The twelfth golden step teaches devotion to the Guru. In the spiritual path, the Guru is more than a teacher. The Guru is a guide, a mirror, and a living embodiment of the truths that the seeker aspires to realize. Without the Guru's light, the path can seem unclear and full of obstacles. With the Guru's guidance, the journey becomes a steady unfolding towards the Divine.

THE ROLE OF THE GURU IN AYYAPPA'S LIFE

Though Ayyappa was a divine being, He honoured the principle of learning from guides and elders. His early training was shaped by wise teachers in martial arts, scriptures and dharma. Even as an avatar, He demonstrated humility and respect for the knowledge passed down through the ages. This example teaches us that seeking and honouring guidance is not a sign of weakness, but of wisdom.

WHY THE GURU IS CENTRAL IN SPIRITUAL LIFE

The human mind is limited in its ability to see beyond its own conditioning. A Guru, having walked the path to realization, can see where the disciple stumbles and where he is strong. The Guru knows when to encourage, when to challenge, and when to allow the student to face life's tests alone.

The Guru is not just a giver of knowledge but a presence that transforms. Sitting in the company of a true Guru can ignite inner clarity without a single word being spoken.

FORMS OF THE GURU

The Guru can take many forms. Sometimes it is a living master who imparts direct guidance. Sometimes a scripture speaks directly to your heart. Sometimes life itself becomes the Guru, teaching through experiences, both joyful and painful. Recognizing the Guru in all these forms requires humility and openness.

DEVOTION AS A TRANSFORMATIVE FORCE

Devotion to the Guru is not blind obedience. It is trust, born of the recognition that the Guru has only the seeker's liberation at heart. This trust allows the disciple to surrender the ego's resistance and open fully to the teachings.

Ayyappa's life reminds us that devotion is an active quality. It is shown through listening with full attention, practising the teachings sincerely, and living in a way that honours the Guru's wisdom.

GURU BHAKTI IN THE VRATA

During the 41-day vrata, the role of the Guru Swamy (the senior devotee leading the group) is central. Pilgrims look to him for guidance in discipline, prayer and conduct. Serving and respecting the Guru Swamy is part of the pilgrimage's inner training. It teaches humility, obedience, and the ability to learn from those who have walked the path before you.

LESSONS FOR MODERN LIFE

In today's age of information, many people believe they can learn everything on their own. While self-study is valuable, there is a profound difference between gathering information and receiving living wisdom. A true Guru transmits not just concepts, but an inner state of being.

In careers, relationships, and personal growth, having a mentor serves the same purpose. They see the bigger picture and can guide you around pitfalls you cannot see for yourself.

CULTIVATING DEVOTION TO THE GURU

- **Choose Wisely:** Seek a Guru whose life reflects the values and truths you aspire to.
- **Serve with Humility:** Offer your time and effort without expectation of reward.
- **Practise the Teachings:** Show devotion through action, not just words.
- **Keep the Connection Alive:** Regularly revisit the Guru's words and presence in your life.

AYYAPPA'S MESSAGE

The Guru is the bridge between the seeker and the Divine. By honouring the Guru, the seeker aligns with the flow of grace and opens the door to inner transformation. Just as Ayyappa respected His teachers and elders, we too must honour those who guide us towards truth.

CLOSING THOUGHT

The twelfth golden step is a reminder that no one walks the path entirely alone. The Guru's light reveals the way, their compassion supports the journey, and their wisdom helps the seeker cross the ocean of illusion. Devotion to the Guru is devotion to the truth that the Guru embodies. By walking in their footsteps, we come closer to walking in the footsteps of the Divine.

GOLDEN STEP THIRTEEN
Self-Discipline

The thirteenth golden step calls the pilgrim to live with self-discipline. Self-discipline is the ability to keep commitments, honour principles, and follow the chosen path with steadiness, regardless of obstacles or temptations. It is the inner strength that allows a person to act according to their values even when emotions, desires, or external pressures urge them otherwise. Without self-discipline, good intentions remain as thoughts and never take shape in action.

Self-discipline is not about harshness towards oneself. It is about choosing the higher good over short-term comfort. It is a form of respect, respect for one's word, one's purpose, and one's relationship with the Divine.

AYYAPPA'S EXAMPLE OF SELF-DISCIPLINE

Ayyappa's life is a shining example of unwavering discipline. From youth, He trained His body and mind to serve His dharma. Whether studying the scriptures, mastering martial skills, or undertaking acts of service, He did not waver from His responsibilities.

One of the clearest demonstrations of His self-discipline was his journey to fetch the milk of the tigress. This task was filled with danger and uncertainty. Ayyappa could have delayed, argued, or sought an easier route, but He did none of these. He took on the mission with full dedication, completing it without complaint or distraction. His focus was not on the difficulty of the task, but on fulfilling the purpose it served.

This level of discipline came from within. It was not enforced by fear of punishment or desire for reward. It flowed naturally from a heart aligned with truth and duty.

THE POWER OF SELF-DISCIPLINE

Self-discipline is the bridge between goals and achievement. It is what turns dreams into reality. Without it, even noble aspirations fade away under the weight of distraction and procrastination. With it, even the most challenging path becomes possible.

Spiritually, self-discipline shapes the mind into a worthy vessel for higher truths. A scattered and undisciplined mind cannot hold deep wisdom for long. Just as a pot must be clean and strong to hold pure water, the mind must be steady and focused to hold the awareness of the Divine.

SELF-DISCIPLINE IN VEDANTA

Vedanta teaches that mastery of the Self is mastery over

the mind and senses. The senses naturally pull towards pleasure and away from discomfort. The undisciplined person becomes a servant to these impulses, constantly shifting with changing moods and desires. The disciplined person, however, is guided by reason and higher purpose, not by momentary urges.

Self-discipline in Vedanta is not suppression but redirection. It is not about rejecting all pleasures but about ensuring that pleasure does not control you. The disciplined seeker chooses actions that serve long-term spiritual growth, even if they require sacrifice in the present moment.

SELF-DISCIPLINE IN THE 41-DAY VRATA

The vrata is one of the most practical trainings in self-discipline. Devotees take on strict vows: simple vegetarian diet, daily prayer, physical restraint, humility in speech, and avoidance of comforts. These are not small adjustments. They require the pilgrim to reshape daily habits, resist cravings, and choose devotion over convenience.

The first days may be the hardest, as the body and mind resist the change. But as the days progress, discipline begins to feel like freedom. By removing unnecessary distractions, the devotee experiences clarity and inner strength. The vrata shows that discipline is not a burden, but a source of deep joy.

MODERN RELEVANCE

In the modern world, distractions are everywhere. Technology offers constant entertainment, advertisements urge us to consume more, and social pressures push us to fit in rather than stay true to our chosen values. Without self-discipline, it is easy to drift through life without ever reaching the deeper purposes we set for ourselves.

Self-discipline is essential for anyone who wishes to live intentionally. For a student, it means sticking to study plans even when friends invite them out. For a professional, it means maintaining integrity in work even when shortcuts seem tempting. For a parent, it means staying patient and consistent in guiding children, even when tired.

In a time when instant gratification is seen as a right, self-discipline becomes a rare and powerful virtue. It allows a person to delay immediate rewards for the sake of something more lasting and meaningful.

HOW TO PRACTISE SELF-DISCIPLINE

- **Set Clear Goals:** Know exactly what you are committing to and why it matters.
- **Create Routines:** Build habits that align with your purpose, so discipline becomes a natural flow rather than a constant struggle.
- **Limit Temptations:** Arrange your environment so that distractions are reduced.
- **Hold Yourself Accountable:** Keep promises to yourself as seriously as promises to others.
- **Start Small:** Build discipline in small daily actions, and let it grow into greater commitments.

THE INNER JOY OF SELF-DISCIPLINE

Though discipline requires effort, it brings a quiet joy that indulgence cannot give. When you live with discipline, you can look back without regret and forward without fear. You know you are walking your chosen path with sincerity.

Self-discipline also deepens self-respect. Each time you honour a commitment, you prove to yourself that your word has power. This builds inner confidence that no external achievement can replace.

AYYAPPA'S MESSAGE

Ayyappa's life reminds us that the disciplined path is the path of freedom. The one who is a slave to impulses may feel free in the moment, but is bound by consequences later. The one who lives with discipline may face effort now, but reaps lasting peace and strength.

For the pilgrim, discipline is not an optional quality. It is the very foundation of the journey. Without it, the steps cannot be climbed. With it, the summit becomes inevitable.

CLOSING THOUGHT

The thirteenth golden step is the step of steadfastness. Self-discipline keeps the pilgrim's feet firmly on the path, regardless of the winds of distraction or difficulty. It transforms good intentions into sacred actions and makes the journey to the Divine not just possible, but certain. In walking this step, you follow in the footsteps of Ayyappa, whose discipline was an unbroken offering to the higher truth.

GOLDEN STEP FOURTEEN
Forgiveness

The fourteenth golden step calls the pilgrim to practise forgiveness, to release resentment, let go of grudges and offer others a fresh chance. Forgiveness is not about denying that wrong was done. It is about freeing the heart from the chains of bitterness and anger. It is a conscious decision to choose peace over vengeance, compassion over judgment.

When we refuse to forgive, we carry the burden of the past into the present. The wound may have been caused years ago, but resentment keeps it alive, robbing us of the joy and clarity we could have today. Forgiveness does not erase the memory, but it transforms the pain into wisdom.

AYYAPPA'S EXAMPLE OF FORGIVENESS

Ayyappa's life reflects a spirit of boundless compassion. Even when misunderstood, opposed or tested by those around Him, He did not respond with anger. His journey to bring the tigress's milk—a task given under false pretences—could have been a cause for resentment. Instead, He treated it as an act of service, showing no bitterness towards those who set the challenge.

In forgiving, Ayyappa displayed a deeper truth: forgiveness is not weakness. It is strength of the highest kind. Anyone can repay hurt with hurt, but only the strong can choose to end the cycle. Forgiveness allowed Ayyappa to act from a place of clarity and love, keeping His mind fixed on dharma rather than revenge.

THE POWER OF FORGIVENESS

Forgiveness is as much a gift to the one who forgives as it is to the one who is forgiven. When we release resentment, we free ourselves from the poison of anger. Holding on to bitterness is like holding on to a burning coal with the intention of throwing it at someone else, but in the process, it burns our own hands.

Forgiveness does not mean trusting blindly or tolerating injustice. It means we stop feeding the emotional energy of hatred. It gives us the strength to set boundaries without the weight of hostility in our hearts.

FORGIVENESS IN VEDANTA

Vedanta teaches that the Self is pure, eternal, and untouched by the faults and mistakes of the ego. When we identify only with the ego, we take every insult and injury personally, clinging to hurt as if it defines us. But when we see ourselves and others as the eternal Self, the actions of the ego are like passing clouds.

In this view, forgiveness becomes natural. We recognize that the one who hurt us acted from ignorance, fear or desire—all products of not knowing the true Self. We may still take practical steps to prevent harm, but in the inner space of the heart, we can let go of the hatred and see the divine essence that lies beyond the outer actions.

FORGIVENESS IN THE 41-DAY VRATA

During the vrata, devotees are encouraged to cultivate purity of thought, word and action. This includes releasing grudges. Carrying anger is a heavy load, and the pilgrimage itself is already physically demanding. Forgiveness lightens the inner journey, making it possible to focus on prayer and devotion.

In the company of fellow pilgrims, small misunderstandings can happen. The discipline of the vrata teaches the pilgrim to resolve these quickly, to seek and offer forgiveness without delay. This not only maintains harmony in the group but also trains the heart to respond with compassion in everyday life.

MODERN RELEVANCE

In today's world, where social and personal conflicts can quickly escalate through words, media and public opinion, forgiveness is often seen as old-fashioned or even naive. Many prefer to 'cancel' rather than reconcile. Yet holding on to anger has not made the world more peaceful, it has only deepened divisions.

Forgiveness is deeply relevant in modern life. It allows families to heal after conflict, friendships to be restored after mistakes, and communities to move forward after injustice. It does not mean forgetting, and it does not remove the need for accountability. But it allows new possibilities to emerge where anger alone would keep doors closed.

In personal relationships, forgiveness breaks the habit of replaying past wrongs in the mind. In workplaces, it helps colleagues work together productively despite disagreements. In society, it helps communities choose dialogue over endless retaliation.

HOW TO PRACTISE FORGIVENESS

- **Acknowledge the Hurt:** Forgiveness does not mean pretending nothing happened. First, face the reality of the harm done.
- **Shift Perspective:** Ask yourself what kind of fears, ignorance or pain might have driven the other person's actions. This does not excuse the act, but it can soften resentment.
- **Release the Desire for Revenge:** Recognize that holding anger will harm you more than it harms the other person.
- **Set Healthy Boundaries:** Forgiveness does not mean allowing continued harm. You can forgive and still protect yourself.
- **Pray for the Other's Growth:** Even if they never apologize, wishing them well can free your heart from the weight of hatred.

THE INNER JOY OF FORGIVENESS

When you forgive, you reclaim your own peace. You no longer need to carry the person who hurt you in your mind every day. You are free to live in the present rather than replay the past. Forgiveness also strengthens compassion. It reminds you that you, too, have made mistakes and needed mercy from others.

The joy of forgiveness is subtle but deep. It is that of a heart that has chosen love over resentment and peace over turmoil. It opens space for healing, for new beginnings, and for a closer connection to the Divine.

AYYAPPA'S MESSAGE

Through His example, Ayyappa shows that forgiveness is not about condoning wrongs but about rising above them. The one who forgives stands in the light while the one who clings to anger stays in shadow. Forgiveness keeps the mind clear, the heart open, and the spirit free to walk the path without unnecessary burdens.

CLOSING THOUGHT

The fourteenth golden step invites you to lay down the weight of the past and step forward unburdened. Forgiveness is not only a gift to others, but also a gift to yourself. When you forgive, you open the door to healing, growth and harmony. You walk in the spirit of Ayyappa, whose compassion was greater than any wrong that could be done to Him. By choosing forgiveness, you make space for grace to work in your life and in the lives of others.

GOLDEN STEP FIFTEEN
Wisdom

The fifteenth golden step calls the pilgrim to cultivate wisdom to see clearly what truly matters and to make choices that reflect that understanding. Wisdom is more than knowledge. It is the ability to apply what we know in a way that leads to peace, harmony and spiritual growth. Many people gather facts, but few live by the deeper truths those facts reveal. Wisdom is not just in the mind. It is in the heart, guiding how we live, speak and act.

When we walk without wisdom, we may run after what glitters but does not last. We may be drawn into conflicts, temptations, and distractions that take us far from our true path. Wisdom helps us step back and ask, 'Will this matter in the long run? Will this bring me closer to my purpose or take me further away?'

AYYAPPA'S EXAMPLE OF WISDOM

Throughout His life, Ayyappa displayed wisdom beyond His

years. He understood that His mission was not to please everyone but to fulfil the divine purpose entrusted to Him. This required seeing through illusions, recognizing the truth in each situation, and choosing the path of dharma even when it was difficult.

One example is His journey for the tigress's milk. While others saw danger and impossibility, Ayyappa saw an opportunity to serve and to demonstrate faith. His wisdom lay not in calculating the odds but in knowing that divine will could accomplish what human reasoning might dismiss. He acted with trust, courage and clarity—qualities that spring from true wisdom.

Ayyappa also knew when to act and when to remain still, when to speak and when to keep silence. This balance is a hallmark of wisdom. It is not just about knowing what to do, but about knowing when and how to do it.

THE POWER OF WISDOM

Wisdom is like a lamp in the darkness. Without it, we may walk quickly but stumble often. With it, even slow steps lead surely to the goal. Wisdom helps us distinguish between what is urgent and what is important, between the fleeting and the eternal.

A wise person does not waste life's precious time on petty quarrels, empty pleasures or endless comparisons. Instead, they invest their energy in what brings real fulfilment, i.e. self-realization, service to others and the cultivation of virtues. Wisdom does not remove life's challenges, but it changes how we meet them.

WISDOM IN VEDANTA

Vedanta teaches that wisdom comes from recognizing the impermanent nature of the world and the eternal nature of the Self. The wise see that material possessions, status and even the body are temporary. This does not mean they reject the world, but they use it as a field for learning and service rather than as the source of ultimate happiness.

True wisdom is to know that our real nature is beyond birth and death, beyond pleasure and pain. When we live with this understanding, we are not easily shaken by life's ups and downs. We still act with compassion and responsibility, but we are anchored in a deeper reality.

WISDOM IN THE 41-DAY VRATA

The vrata offers many opportunities to practise wisdom. The discipline of waking early, bathing in cold water, eating simple food and controlling speech may seem small, but each act trains the mind to choose long-term benefit over short-term comfort.

Wisdom in the vrata is also about avoiding unnecessary arguments, focusing on prayer rather than gossip, and remembering the sacred purpose behind each ritual. The wise pilgrim does not measure success by comfort but by how much closer the journey brings him to the Lord.

MODERN RELEVANCE

In today's fast-moving world, we are surrounded by information but not always by wisdom. Technology gives us instant access to news, opinions and data, but without discernment, we can become overwhelmed or misled. Wisdom helps us filter what is worth our attention and what is simply noise.

In careers, wisdom means choosing work that aligns with our values rather than chasing titles or salaries alone. In relationships, it means looking beyond surface attractions to the qualities that build trust and harmony. In daily life, it means pausing before reacting, and considering whether our actions will create peace or conflict.

Without wisdom, even great intelligence can lead to poor choices. With wisdom, even simple actions can become powerful steps towards a meaningful life.

HOW TO PRACTISE WISDOM

- **Reflect Daily:** Spend time each day in quiet thought or meditation, asking what really matters and how you can live by it.
- **Learn from Experience:** See every success and failure as a lesson. Ask what it is teaching you about yourself and about life.
- **Seek Guidance:** Listen to the advice of teachers, elders and scriptures, but test it against your own experience and conscience.
- **Pause before Acting:** A moment of reflection can prevent a lifetime of regret.
- **Align Actions with Values:** Let your choices reflect what you truly believe, not just what is convenient or popular.

THE INNER JOY OF WISDOM

Wisdom brings a calm strength. It frees you from being tossed about by every new trend, fear or temptation. When you know what truly matters, you can let go of what does not serve your higher purpose. This gives you more time, more energy and more peace.

The joy of wisdom is the joy of living in harmony with truth. It is the quiet satisfaction of knowing you are moving in the right direction, even if the journey is long. It is the confidence of acting with integrity, regardless of what others may think.

AYYAPPA'S MESSAGE

Ayyappa's life reminds us that wisdom is not the result of clever arguments or endless study alone. It is the fruit of humility, devotion and a willingness to learn from every moment. It is seeing the hand of the Divine in all situations and choosing to walk in step with it.

CLOSING THOUGHT

The fifteenth golden step invites you to walk with open eyes and a clear heart. Wisdom does not remove life's challenges, but it ensures that every choice moves you closer to the light. In choosing wisely, you honour both yourself and the Divine. With each step guided by wisdom, the path becomes clearer, the burdens lighter, and the destination certain.

GOLDEN STEP SIXTEEN
Courage

The sixteenth golden step calls the pilgrim to live with the courage to act according to dharma, even when it is hard, risky or unpopular. Courage is not the absence of fear. It is the strength to do what is right despite fear. It is the steady flame that keeps burning when storms threaten to put it out.

Without courage, even the best intentions remain unfulfilled. Many know the right path but hesitate to walk it because of uncertainty, criticism or hardship. Courage bridges the gap between knowing and doing. It transforms noble thoughts into noble actions.

AYYAPPA'S EXAMPLE OF COURAGE

Ayyappa's life is a tapestry woven with acts of courage. From the moment of His divine birth, His mission was to protect and guide. One of the most remembered examples is His journey for the tigress's milk. This task was not only dangerous but seemed impossible to those around Him. Yet Ayyappa stepped forward without complaint. His courage was not reckless bravado. It was the quiet confidence that comes from knowing one is acting in harmony with divine will.

Even in times when others doubted or opposed Him, Ayyappa remained steadfast. He did not let fear of failure, danger or disapproval sway His actions. His courage was anchored in faith and guided by wisdom, ensuring it did not turn into arrogance or stubbornness.

THE POWER OF COURAGE

Courage is the key that unlocks many other virtues. Without it, compassion can remain silent in the face of injustice. Without it, truthfulness can be abandoned when lies feel safer. Without it, discipline can fade when temptations grow strong. Courage empowers the pilgrim to stand firm, not only in grand moments of challenge but also in daily situations that test integrity.

It takes courage to admit mistakes, to forgive when the hurt is deep, to let go of harmful habits, and to choose a simpler life in a world that prizes excess. It takes courage to be different when the crowd moves in another direction.

COURAGE IN VEDANTA

Vedanta teaches that the root of fear is ignorance of our true nature. When we identify only with the body and mind, we feel small, vulnerable and easily threatened. But when we realize that our essence is the eternal Self, untouched by birth or death, fear begins to dissolve.

This spiritual understanding creates a courage that is not dependent on outer circumstances. It allows the pilgrim to face life's uncertainties with calm resolve. True courage is not about forcing our will upon the world. It is about aligning with truth and trusting the outcome to the Divine.

COURAGE IN THE 41-DAY VRATA

The vrata trains courage in subtle ways. Waking before dawn on cold mornings requires courage to overcome the pull of comfort. Choosing to speak gently when irritated requires courage to master the tongue. Walking barefoot over rough paths and sleeping with little luxury requires courage to endure discomfort without complaint.

On the pilgrimage to Sabarimala, courage is also needed in moments of physical challenge, such as climbing steep hills or walking long distances. But more than the body, it is the mind that is trained to stay focused on the goal despite fatigue, distractions or doubt.

MODERN RELEVANCE

In today's world, courage takes many forms. It may mean speaking up against wrongdoing at work even if it risks your position. It may mean choosing an ethical but less profitable path in business. It may mean ending habits that keep you from your higher purpose, even when those habits feel safe and familiar.

Social pressures often push people to blend in rather than stand apart. The courage to live by your values may make you seem unusual to others, but it also inspires respect and trust. Courage does not mean being loud or forceful. Sometimes the most courageous act is a quiet refusal to compromise your principles.

For young people, courage might mean resisting peer pressure and making choices that protect their well-being and future. For parents, it may mean guiding children with firmness and love even when they resist. For leaders, it may mean putting the welfare of others before personal gain.

HOW TO PRACTISE COURAGE

- **Strengthen Faith:** Trust that when you act in harmony with dharma, you are supported by the Divine, even if the path is difficult.
- **Start Small:** Face small fears daily, speaking the truth in gentle ways, taking on challenges you would usually avoid, or saying no when it matters.
- **Prepare the Mind:** Meditation and self-reflection build inner stability so you can face challenges without panic.
- **Stay Aligned with Values:** Let your decisions be guided by what is right, not just by what is easy or popular.
- **Accept Discomfort:** Growth often requires stepping outside the comfort zone. Welcome the unease as a sign you are stretching beyond limits.

THE INNER JOY OF COURAGE

Courage brings a deep inner freedom. When you are no longer ruled by fear, you can act with authenticity and clarity. You do not need to pretend or hide behind masks. You can meet life openly, ready to respond to whatever comes.

This freedom also brings peace. Decisions become simpler when they are based on what is right rather than on avoiding discomfort or judgment. Even if the outcome is not what you hoped for, you rest knowing that you acted with integrity.

AYYAPPA'S MESSAGE

Through His life, Ayyappa teaches that courage is not a rare quality meant only for heroes in grand tales. It is a daily necessity for anyone who seeks to live with truth and devotion. Each choice to follow dharma, each act of kindness in the face of hostility, each step taken in faith rather than fear are all acts of courage.

CLOSING THOUGHT

The sixteenth golden step reminds us that courage is the guardian of all other virtues. Without it, wisdom may remain unused, compassion unspoken, and truth unshared. With it, the path becomes one of steady progress, no matter how steep the climb. Courage does not promise an easy journey, but it ensures that every step is taken with strength, dignity and unwavering faith in the light of the Divine.

GOLDEN STEP SEVENTEEN

Devotion to God

The seventeenth golden step is about complete devotion to God. In Sanskrit, this is called *bhakti*. Devotion is not limited to rituals or formal worship. It is the inner condition of the heart that is always aware of the Divine and is in harmony with that awareness.

THE ESSENCE OF DEVOTION

True devotion is unconditional. It does not bargain with God for rewards, nor does it turn away in times of difficulty. It is love for the Divine simply because God is the source and essence of all that is. This love transforms every action, every word, and every thought into an offering.

Devotion is the bridge between the human and the Divine. Even when the mind is restless and full of doubts, devotion can lead the seeker forward because the heart can sometimes reach where the intellect cannot.

AYYAPPA'S DEVOTION

Swamy Ayyappa's entire life was an act of devotion. His mission was carried out in service to the will of the Divine. His compassion for all beings was a reflection of His connection to the Supreme. Whether He was in the midst of the forest, on a journey to help others, or in the act of establishing the Sabarimala temple, His actions flowed from love for the divine presence.

DEVOTION IN THE LIFE OF A PILGRIM

For an Ayyappa devotee, devotion begins to deepen during the 41-day vrata. Each day of discipline, prayer and humility strengthens the bond between the devotee and the Lord. The journey to Sabarimala becomes more than a physical pilgrimage. It becomes a symbolic walk towards God, step by step, with every moment an act of surrender.

The chanting of *Swamiye Sharanam Ayyappa* during the journey is a constant reminder of reliance on the Divine. This chant is not only a call for protection but also a declaration of trust.

FORMS OF DEVOTION

Devotion can be expressed in many ways:

- **Prayer and Chanting:** Offering words of praise and remembrance.
- **Service to Others:** Seeing God in every person and helping without expectation.

- **Meditation:** Directing the mind towards the Divine in silence.
- **Surrender:** Trusting in God's will even when life is uncertain.
- **Gratitude:** Recognizing every moment and every blessing as a gift from God.

DEVOTION IN MODERN LIFE

In a world full of distractions, devotion provides a steady anchor. It prevents the heart from being consumed by materialism and constant comparison. Devotion also creates resilience because one who trusts in God is not easily shaken by changes in life.

For today's youth, devotion can be integrated into daily life through simple but consistent acts. This may be a morning prayer, an evening reflection, a few minutes of chanting during the day, or dedicating work and studies to a higher purpose.

AYYAPPA'S MESSAGE

Devotion is not weakness. It is a source of immense strength because it connects you to an infinite source of love and wisdom. It transforms ordinary life into a spiritual journey.

CLOSING THOUGHT

The seventeenth golden step teaches that devotion is the lifeblood of the spiritual path. It is the warmth that melts pride, removes doubt, and its strength carries the seeker through every challenge. A devotee who walks with unwavering love for God finds joy not only in the temple but also in every moment of life. Just as Ayyappa's life was a song of devotion, so too can ours be when the heart rests in the Divine.

GOLDEN STEP EIGHTEEN
Union with God

The eighteenth golden step is the final and highest stage of the spiritual journey. It represents complete union with God, where the seeker realizes their true nature as one with the Divine. This is the culmination of all the previous steps, where devotion, discipline, humility, service, truth and compassion merge into a single experience of oneness.

THE MEANING OF UNION

Union with God is not about going somewhere or gaining something new. It is the realization that you have always been connected to the Divine, that your deepest self is not separate from the source of all creation. This truth is expressed in the great Vedantic statement *Tat Tvam Asi.*

When this truth is understood, life changes completely. Fear disappears because you know you are eternal. Hatred dissolves because you see the same divine essence in every being. The restless search for meaning ends because you have found the centre of all meaning within yourself.

AYYAPPA'S STATE OF UNION

Swamy Ayyappa lived in constant awareness of His oneness with the Divine. His life was an example of perfect balance between action in the world and inner union with God. Even when facing challenges, He acted from a place of peace and clarity because His identity was rooted in the Supreme.

When He established Sabarimala as a place of pilgrimage, it was not simply to honour His own journey but to provide a path for others to discover their own union with God. Each of the 18 steps is a stage of purification leading to this realization.

THE PILGRIM'S EXPERIENCE

For the devotee, reaching the eighteenth step at Sabarimala is a deeply symbolic moment. After the long journey, the hardships of the 41-day vrata, and the climb up the sacred path, the devotee reaches the sanctum. Bowing before Lord Ayyappa at this point is not merely a physical act but the surrender of the ego. The Self that thought it was separate dissolves in the presence of the Infinite.

The journey to this point reflects the inner journey of every human being. Life itself is a pilgrimage, and the goal is not only to reach a temple on a hill but also to awaken to the temple within.

UNION IN DAILY LIFE

Union with God is not something that exists only in moments of meditation or worship. It is a state that can permeate every action. When you see the Divine in the people you meet, in the work you do, in the challenges you face, you are living in union.

This state of awareness transforms how you interact with the world. You no longer see life as divided between sacred and ordinary. Every moment becomes sacred, and the ordinary becomes extraordinary.

THE RELEVANCE FOR MODERN TIMES

In today's world, where people are often pulled in many directions, the realization of oneness can bring profound peace. It removes the feeling of isolation and competition that so often drives stress and conflict. Instead, you begin to live from a place of connection and purpose.

Union with God also changes how we relate to others. When you see the same divine light in all, discrimination and prejudice lose their power. This is why Sabarimala stands as a beacon where caste, religion and all forms of separation disappear.

AYYAPPA'S FINAL LESSON

The eighteenth golden step is not the end of the journey but the beginning of a new way of living. Once you have realized your oneness with the Divine, every step you take in life is an expression of that truth.

Ayyappa's message is that this union is not reserved for saints or sages. It is the birthright of every human being. The path may be long and require discipline, but the destination is certain for those who persevere.

CLOSING THOUGHT

The eighteenth golden step teaches that the highest goal of life is to know your true Self as one with God. This realization is freedom, joy and peace beyond measure. When you stand in this awareness, the world no longer feels like a place to conquer or escape from. It becomes a place to love, serve and celebrate. Just as a river finds its home in the ocean, so too does the soul find its home in the boundless presence of the Divine.

PATH OF THE PRACTICE

Bringing Ayyappa's Wisdom Home

A Powerful Practical Companion for Today's Youth

PROLOGUE

Why Sabarimala Matters Now

Sabarimala is more than a destination. It is a blueprint for living with strength, clarity and compassion in a noisy, divided world. Ayyappa is the teacher who walks beside you through exams, office deadlines, family responsibilities and moments of self-doubt. The 18 golden steps are not only granite beneath a pilgrim's feet. They are inner thresholds that reshape how you think, choose, love and serve.

At Sabarimala, strangers greet each other as Swamy. This is not flattery. It is Vedanta made practical. *Tat Tvam Asi.* The Divine lives in you, and in everyone you meet. This single insight cuts through caste, class, gender, and all other labels that usually harden hearts. The forest path to the shrine is a reminder that life is a pilgrimage of the heart. Every step matters.

This companion section gathers the essence of all 18 steps into one integrated manual. It blends stories from Ayyappa's life and the pilgrimage tradition, Vedantic guidance, and modern practices you can use today. Read it slowly. Try one practice a day. Discuss with friends. Bring it to your workplace, your team, your family. Treat it as a living book that grows with you.

PART I

Ayyappa's Life Lessons for Today's Seeker

1. BORN OF SHIVA AND MOHINI, BORN FOR PURPOSE

Ayyappa, the child of Shiva and Mohini, is not a figure of accident or coincidence. His very birth carries a mission to protect dharma, to uplift the vulnerable, and to remind the world that strength and compassion are not opposites but two halves of the same jewel.

As Manikandan, the boy-prince, He grows up in a royal household surrounded by the comforts and temptations of power, yet His heart remains free from attachment to the throne. He learns archery with the same diligence with which He learns music. He studies sword craft without losing His love for scripture. He watches His teachers and elders closely, learning not just the skills they teach but also the way they carry themselves in moments of tension.

The lesson here is timeless: your skill is only complete

when it is guided by kindness. You can write flawless code without humiliating a junior developer. You can argue in court without belittling the opposing counsel. You can run a company and still listen with patience to your child's long story about school.

MODERN PRACTICE TIP

- Choose one skill you are good at and practise pairing it with kindness. For example, if you are a strong negotiator, aim to close a deal where both sides walk away feeling respected.
- Once a week, pause and ask yourself: 'Am I using my abilities to build or to dominate?'

Story: A young tech manager once asked his mentor how to rise faster in his career. The mentor replied, 'Be the person everyone trusts when the stakes are high. That is worth more than any promotion list.' Ayyappa's childhood was training for exactly that—to be trusted in every storm.

2. THE CRY OF THE KINGDOM AND THE FOREST ANSWER

When Mahishi's tyranny threatens the kingdom, Ayyappa does not react in haste. He does not gather an army overnight or shout for immediate war. Instead, He listens. He studies the lay of the land, the fears of the people, and the hidden strengths that could be brought forward.

The forest He enters is not just a battlefield waiting to happen. It is a place of training, reflection and deep listening. The rustle of leaves teaches patience. The flowing river teaches renewal. The quietness forces the mind to face itself.

MODERN PRACTICE TIP

- When faced with a problem, resist the urge to react instantly. Spend a day or even a few hours in 'listening mode', gathering facts, perspectives and understanding before deciding.
- Take a walk without your phone at least once a week. Let nature re-teach you the skill of observation.

Story: A social worker in Kerala faced a community dispute over water sharing. Instead of calling for a meeting right away, she spent three days visiting each family quietly. When the meeting finally happened, everyone felt heard and the solution was accepted in one sitting. That was a modern echo of Ayyappa's forest preparation.

3. THE SLAYING OF MAHISHI AND THE INNER BATTLE

The battle with Mahishi is not just an episode in myth. It is a living parable about conquering inner demons. Mahishi represents uncontrolled anger, greed, envy and the restless craving that drives people to harm others. Ayyappa's victory is not won through reckless violence but through disciplined mastery of mind and skill.

MODERN PRACTICE TIP

- Identify your Mahishi, the habit or thought pattern that most pulls you away from your best self.
- When it arises, pause and breathe deeply three times before acting. This pause can be your first victory.

Story: A man trying to quit smoking once said, 'Every time I feel the urge, I tell myself this is the moment to slay my Mahishi.' Over a year, those small moments of victory built into complete freedom from the habit. The battlefield can be your own living room, your own mind.

4. VAVAR AND THE VOW OF FRIENDSHIP

The friendship between Ayyappa and Vavar, the Muslim warrior, is a reminder that dharma does not belong to one label or boundary. This was not tolerance but mutual respect, active and alive. Vavar's shrine still stands near the pilgrimage route as a sign that true strength sees beyond religion, caste and culture.

MODERN PRACTICE TIP

- Make a conscious effort to respect the dignity of someone whose background or beliefs differ from yours.
- Work on one joint project or act of service with a person from a different faith or worldview.

Story: A Hindu shopkeeper and a Muslim mechanic in Pathanamthitta agreed to close their shops for each other's festivals. They lost no customers. Instead, they gained more loyalty because they modelled the same friendship that Ayyappa and Vavar lived.

5. MALIKAPPURATHAMMA AND THE SACREDNESS OF A VOW

Ayyappa's choice to remain a *naishtika brahmachari* is a commitment to focused devotion. The presence of Malikappurathamma at the shrine honours divine feminine power and reminds pilgrims that keeping a vow shapes the soul. A promise, when kept, becomes a force that builds trust in the Self and in others.

MODERN PRACTICE TIP

- Choose one small vow you can keep for 41 days. For example, avoiding gossip, waking at a fixed time for prayer, or eating with mindfulness.
- Track your progress on paper to strengthen your sense of accountability.

Story: A student once vowed to meditate for five minutes every morning before opening his phone. Over time, the five minutes became 20, and he found himself calmer in every exam season. The size of the vow matters less than the sincerity with which it is kept.

6. THE 18 GOLDEN STEPS AS INNER THRESHOLDS

The 18 steps at Sabarimala are more than stone and metal. They are an inner staircase, each one representing a quality or practice to be lived. Climbing them at the temple is a ritual. Climbing them in daily life is transformation.

MODERN PRACTICE TIP

- Choose one step each week to focus on in your life: truthfulness, patience, devotion, and so on.
- Write one action you will take each day to live that step. Review at the week's end before moving to the next.

Story: A pilgrim who could not physically visit Sabarimala one year decided to 'walk the steps' from home. Each day he lived out one of the steps intentionally. By the eighteenth day, he said the change in his thinking and speech was more powerful than any trip he had taken before.

PART II

The 41 Day Vrata, a Training Camp for the Soul

The vrata is a training camp for the mind and heart. Simple food, early rising, bathing, clean living, abstinence, service, prayer and the constant remembrance of *Swamiye Sharanam Ayyappa* shape a new rhythm inside you. You learn that comfort does not define you. Purpose does.

1. WHY SIMPLICITY WORKS

Simplicity clears friction. When food is simple, sleep is simple and speech is simple, the mind gets space to breathe. You realize how much energy goes into managing preferences and reactions. The vrata gives that energy back to your purpose. A simple plate of rice and dal, eaten with attention, becomes sacred. A simple set of clothes frees you from the endless loop of appearance anxiety. A simple schedule makes room for deep work, deep rest and deep prayer.

2. IRUMUDI AND THE ART OF CARRYING WELL

The irumudi on a devotee's head is a living teaching. Life will ask you to carry responsibilities. Carry them with dignity, clarity and prayer. When your burden is consecrated, it stops feeling like a burden. It becomes an offering. Students can write the subject they fear most on a small paper, place it near their study space and whisper, 'I carry you with faith.' Professionals can treat their toughest project as an offering, not a punishment. Parents can hold their daily chores as love in motion.

3. PAMBA AND THE RIVER OF RENEWAL

The river bath before the climb is an enactment of inner cleansing. You leave behind pettiness, resentment and self-obsession. You ask for the strength to climb with kindness. You remember that renewal is always available if you are willing to begin again. At home, a cool shower before evening prayer can become your Pamba. Let the water carry away the day's heat so that you can meet your family with freshness.

4. CLIMBING WITH OTHERS, LEARNING TO BELONG

Pilgrims move in groups led by a Guru Swamy. In that small community, you learn to wait for the slow walker, to encourage the doubtful, to share food, and to laugh together. You see who you become when you are tired. You see how others carry you when you are weak. In a world that often worships hyper-individualism, the pilgrimage shows that belonging is power. Belonging is also a discipline. You show up on time, you carry your share, you ask for help before you break.

5. THE STEPS AND THE SILENCE

The Pathinettampadi demand humility. You climb with folded hands, with gratitude, with the awareness that millions have climbed before you and millions more will come after you. In that humility, your personal story opens into a larger story. Silence is not empty in that space. It is full of presence. In daily life, let your steps up a staircase at home remind you to pause for one breath of gratitude at each landing.

6. A DAY BY DAY CITY VRATA

You can bring the hills to your routine. Here is a detailed 41-day plan that blends discipline and grace.

- Day 1. Begin with a clean space. Declutter your room, set a small altar with a lamp or a picture of Ayyappa. Whisper your vow aloud.
- Day 2. Wake before sunrise. Cold or cool bath. Light the lamp and chant your chosen mantra 108 times. Keep meals simple.
- Day 3. Write a letter of gratitude to your parents or

guardians. If they are not present or safe to contact, write and place it at your altar.

- Day 4. Practise silence for one hour. No music, no chatter, only breath and awareness.
- Day 5. Service day. Offer one hour to help someone without being asked.
- Day 6. Digital boundary. Keep your phone away for the first hour after waking and the last hour before sleep.
- Day 7. Forgiveness check. Write one apology you owe. If possible, deliver it kindly.
- Day 8. Food mindfulness. Eat one meal in silence, thanking each person who made it possible, from farmer to cook.
- Day 9. Study session. Choose a sacred text or the life of a saint. Read two pages and note one line to carry.
- Day 10. Body care. Stretch, walk or do yoga for 30 minutes as an offering, not as vanity.
- Day 11. Speech discipline. For one day, do not complain. Replace a complaint with a helpful action.
- Day 12. Nature time. Spend 30 minutes with a tree or a river. Listen more than you speak.
- Day 13. Mentor moment. Encourage a younger student or colleague. Share a useful resource.
- Day 14. Financial honesty. Track your spending for one day and give a small portion to a cause that uplifts.
- Day 15. Reconciliation. Reach out to a friend with whom you lost touch. Offer warmth without agenda.
- Day 16. Creative devotion. Sing, draw or write a small hymn to the Divine.
- Day 17. Breath practice. Box breathing. Inhale four, hold four, exhale four, hold four. Repeat for five minutes.

- Day 18. Work as worship. Do your main task today with full attention. No multitasking.
- Day 19. Pilgrim walk. Take a slow walk and synchronize your steps with breath. If you can, walk barefoot on grass.
- Day 20. *Annadanam* at home. Cook or buy a meal for someone who needs it. Serve with dignity.
- Day 21. Reflection. Journal on where you feel most reactive and how you can respond instead.
- Day 22. Teach what you learn. Share one insight from your readings with a friend.
- Day 23. Restraint. Choose one indulgence and abstain today with joy.
- Day 24. Joy practice. Laugh with a child, play a sport or dance alone. Offer your joy to God.
- Day 25. Boundaries. Write your top three values. Say no to one request that violates them.
- Day 26. Courage. Do one thing you have been avoiding that is good for you.
- Day 27. Listening. Call an elder and ask for a story from their youth. Listen without rushing.
- Day 28. Study deeper. Learn the meaning of *Tat Tvam Asi* and write your own explanation in one page.
- Day 29. Healing. If there is a wound you carry, speak to a trusted mentor or counsellor today.
- Day 30. Clean wealth. Earn, save and give with honesty. Review your finances with integrity.
- Day 31. Silence retreat. Spend half a day offline and in quiet activities.
- Day 32. Art of saying thank you. Write five thank you messages and send them.

- Day 33. Relationship repair. If safe, have a truth with kindness conversation with someone important.
- Day 34. Community *seva*. Join a group activity that helps your neighbourhood.
- Day 35. Study circle. Invite two friends to read a page with you and discuss.
- Day 36. Clean inputs. Curate your media feed. Unfollow what clouds your mind.
- Day 37. Deep work. Set a timer for four sprints of 25 minutes and create something meaningful.
- Day 38. Evening prayer. Offer the day to Ayyappa. Sing or listen to *Harivarasanam*.
- Day 39. Gratitude marathon. Write 15 things you are grateful for, specific and honest.
- Day 40. Big picture. Walk under the open sky and remember you are part of something vast and kind.
- Day 41. Renewal. Renew your vow for the next season. Choose one lasting habit to carry forward.

PART III

Tat Tvam Asi, Made Practical for Modern Life

Tat Tvam Asi means your deepest identity is divine. It does not make you arrogant. It makes you responsible. If the same light shines in all, you cannot exploit, belittle or ignore others. You cannot pollute rivers or the mind. You cannot hide from your potential. You are called to live in a way that honours this light.

1. STUDY, WORK AND EXCELLENCE

Do your task as worship. Excellence with humility becomes your signature. A student who studies as service learns faster because anxiety loosens its grip. A coder who writes clean code as an offering takes joy in clarity. A nurse who changes a bandage as if serving God in that bed feels no task as low. A manager who mentors the weakest link lifts the whole team. *Tat Tvam Asi* is not a theory. It is a posture that transforms the smallest actions.

2. RELATIONSHIPS AS SACRED PRACTICE

See the sacred in each person. Speak to that sacredness with honesty and care. When tension rises, remind yourself that the person in front of you is a traveller like you, learning to love through mistakes. Boundaries protect love. Honesty clarifies love. Patience matures love. *Tat Tvam Asi* shines in listening without defence and in speaking without attack. Love that is wise does not enable harm. It invites growth.

3. CONFLICT, A FIELD FOR GROWTH

The other is not your enemy. The problem is your shared enemy. Solve it together. Name the issue, not the person. Propose one step that serves both. If tempers rise, take a two-minute pause and resume with a calmer voice. You respect your own dignity and theirs. This approach turns conflict into a teacher rather than a trap.

4. MENTAL HEALTH WITH VEDANTIC CLARITY

You are not your worst day. You are not your worst thought. You are not your diagnosis. You are awareness in which these states rise and fall. This does not deny therapy or medication. It supports them. The witness perspective gives space. With space comes choice. With choice comes healing. Saying 'I am awareness', and 'I am having a panic wave' is more freeing than saying 'I am panic'. Seek help when needed. Accept help as grace, not as weakness.

5. SELF-TALK THAT HEALS

Stop insulting yourself. Speak to yourself as you would to a beloved child who is learning to walk. Firm, kind and clear. Replace 'what is wrong with me' with 'what is my next right step'. Replace 'I failed again' with 'I learnt one more way not to do it'. Replace 'I am alone' with 'I am carried by grace and I can ask for support'.

PART IV

Practical Steps on the 18 Steps as a Full Life Practice

The sacred 18 steps at Sabarimala are not only a physical ascent to the sanctum of Lord Ayyappa, but also a profound inner journey. Each step represents a principle or value that, when practised, leads the seeker closer to self-realization. The steps are symbolic and they can be practised daily, wherever you are. Below is a detailed guide to making them a complete life practice.

STEP 1: RENUNCIATION

Choose one habit, attachment or distraction that drains your spiritual focus and let it go. Start small, such as reducing entertainment time or avoiding gossip. Replace that space with prayer, reading scripture or seva. Notice how light you feel when you do not cling to what you do not need. Over time, increase the scope of what you are ready to release.

STEP 2: CONTROL OF THE SENSES

Learn to pause before reacting to temptations of sight, sound, taste, smell and touch. For example, practise mindful eating, avoid unnecessary scrolling on your phone and listen deeply when someone speaks. Spend a day each week consciously limiting sensory input to re-train your mind. Direct the senses towards uplifting sights, sounds and experiences that strengthen your vrata.

STEP 3: PURITY OF MIND

Keep your thoughts clean by watching them closely and replacing negativity with prayer or blessings. If you catch yourself judging someone, immediately think of a good quality they have. Read or listen to spiritually inspiring content daily. Avoid environments that fill your mind with anger, lust, or greed. Start and end each day with a few minutes of quiet reflection.

STEP 4: TRUTHFULNESS

Commit to speaking only what is true, kind, and beneficial. Avoid exaggeration or half-truths even in casual conversation. When unsure whether to speak, remain silent until you can choose your words wisely. Align your actions with your words so people can trust you fully. Review your day and note if you drifted from truth, then correct it.

STEP 5: COMPASSION

Look for opportunities each day to help without expecting anything in return. It could be a smile, a listening ear or a small act of service. Remember that compassion is also shown in patience and understanding. If you hear of someone struggling, silently pray for their well-being. Serve where there is need, even in small, unnoticed ways.

STEP 6: HUMILITY

See every person as equally valuable in the eyes of God. Do tasks without seeking praise, whether it is cleaning, cooking or carrying burdens. Remember that service is sacred when done quietly. Avoid boasting about your actions. Practise bowing to elders, saints and even nature, acknowledging the divine in all.

STEP 7: PATIENCE

When delays or challenges arise, breathe deeply and accept them as part of the journey. Use waiting times for chanting or reflection instead of irritation. Avoid rushing through tasks; do them steadily and well. Remember that some fruits take time to ripen. End each day by recalling a moment you stayed calm instead of reacting hastily.

STEP 8: PERSEVERANCE

Do not abandon your commitment when enthusiasm fades. Continue daily practices, like prayers, reading or physical preparations for the pilgrimage, even on difficult days. Break large goals into smaller steps so they feel achievable. When faced with setbacks, remind yourself why you started. Trust that steady effort brings lasting results.

STEP 9: DETACHMENT FROM MATERIALISM

Enjoy the comforts you have without clinging to them. Skip one purchase each week and use the money for charity or seva. Avoid constant comparisons with others' possessions. Use and care for your belongings, but remember they are temporary. Practise gratitude for simple things like fresh air, water, and the sky above.

STEP 10: GRATITUDE

Start and end each day by naming three blessings you have received. Thank people for their service, even in small ways like a shopkeeper handing your change. Look for the good hidden within challenges. Keep a gratitude diary to remind yourself of life's richness. Speak your thanks aloud to God in prayer.

STEP 11: CONTENTMENT

Each day, pause to enjoy what is already present instead of chasing the next desire. Eat with awareness and savour every bite. Notice the comfort of your home, the kindness of friends, or the gift of health. Avoid overloading your schedule with constant striving. Let your heart rest in the peace of 'enough.'

STEP 12: DEVOTION TO THE GURU

Follow at least one instruction of your Guru with sincerity and consistency. Study their teachings regularly, not just when convenient. Offer a small prayer of gratitude to the Guru daily. When in doubt, think about what your Guru would advise. Serve the Guru's mission in whatever way you can.

STEP 13: SELF-DISCIPLINE

Fulfil your commitments without excuses. Keep a fixed time for prayers or meditation and stick to it daily. Avoid temptations that lead you off your path. Make a written plan for your day and follow it. Remember that discipline in small things builds strength for greater challenges.

STEP 14: FORGIVENESS

Think of one person you hold resentment towards and silently wish them well. Understand that holding anger harms you more than the other person. Let go of the past each night before sleeping. Practise forgiving small irritations quickly so they do not grow. Remember that forgiveness does not excuse wrongdoing but frees your heart.

STEP 15: WISDOM

Before acting, ask yourself if the decision will matter in a year's time. Read scripture or the words of saints to sharpen your understanding. Seek advice from elders before making big choices. Learn from your mistakes instead of repeating them. Value time and energy by investing them in what truly matters.

STEP 16: COURAGE

Do what is right even if it is difficult or unpopular. Speak up for truth with respect and clarity. Face your fears one small step at a time. Remember that courage grows with each act of righteousness. Keep faith that God's strength will carry you through.

STEP 17: DEVOTION TO GOD

Dedicate your actions to God, whether you are working, walking or resting. Chant the divine name during routine activities. Visit a temple or sacred place regularly. Offer food, flowers or prayers with love. Remember God's presence in every moment, not just during rituals.

STEP 18: UNION WITH GOD

Spend a few minutes daily in silent meditation, feeling your oneness with the Divine. Reflect on how all beings share the same sacred source. See God's presence in nature, people, and even in challenges. Surrender your will to God's plan. Live each day as if every act is an offering to the Supreme.

INTEGRATING THE STEPS INTO DAILY LIFE

Create a 'Step Calendar' where each day you focus on one step in depth, cycling through all 18 steps in about three weeks. Keep a notebook to reflect on how each value shows up in your day.

By practising the steps intentionally, you transform your daily life into a Sabarimala pilgrimage, a constant ascent towards the Divine.

PART V

Pilgrim Stories to Walk by

1. THE SCEPTIC WHO BECAME A SERVANT

Rajesh was a corporate executive in Bengaluru. He was known among friends as a sharp, analytical man who dismissed anything he could not measure or quantify. Religion, to him, was simply tradition and superstition. One year, after persistent invitations from an old school friend, he reluctantly agreed to join a pilgrimage to Sabarimala.

From the very first day of the 41-day vrata, he felt out of place. The simple clothing, the vegetarian diet, the daily prayers, these were so far removed from his usual routine that he almost quit on the second day. But he stayed, partly to avoid letting his friend down.

Something began to shift during the journey. The group's humility impressed him, strangers offering food to strangers, young men touching the feet of elders they had never met, and the constant chanting of *Swamiye Sharanam Ayyappa* which seemed to keep spirits high even when they were exhausted.

The turning point came on the long forest path to Sabarimala. A barefoot old man stumbled and fell on the rocky trail. Rajesh, without thinking, rushed forward to help him. The man looked into his eyes and said, 'You are serving Ayyappa Himself when you serve others.' For reasons Rajesh could not explain, tears filled his eyes. In that moment, the idea that divinity could be found in selfless service made sense to him in a way no argument ever could.

When he reached the temple and saw the idol of Lord Ayyappa, Rajesh did not pray for wealth or success. He simply prayed, 'Make me a servant.' From that year onward, he returned to Sabarimala annually, not to seek blessings but to serve food and water to tired pilgrims along the path.

Message: Sometimes faith begins not with belief, but with action. Service can open the heart where logic cannot.

2. THE MOTHER WHO WALKED FOR HER SON

Lakshmi was a schoolteacher from a small village in Tamil Nadu. Her son, Arun, had been bedridden for years with a rare illness that left him too weak to walk more than a few steps. The family had exhausted their savings on treatments and prayed at countless temples. A neighbour suggested she take a vow to Lord Ayyappa and walk to Sabarimala.

Lakshmi decided to do the 41-day vrata with complete dedication. She rose before sunrise each day, bathed in cold water, offered prayers, and chanted the Lord's name while cooking, working and caring for her son. When the day came for the journey, she joined a small group from her village, carrying her irumudi on her head and walking barefoot.

The trek was gruelling. At one steep section, Lakshmi's legs trembled from fatigue. She silently told Ayyappa, 'I will not stop until I see You, because my child needs You.' That night, in a pilgrim shelter, she dreamt of a young man in black garments giving her water and telling her, 'Your son will walk with you next year.'

When she returned home, Arun's health slowly improved. Within a year, he could walk unassisted. True to the dream, mother and son made the pilgrimage together the next year. Lakshmi said she felt no surprise, only gratitude.

Message: Devotion fuelled by love can move mountains, and sometimes the answer to a prayer comes in stages, preparing both the devotee and the blessing.

3. THE STRANGER WHO CARRIED MY BURDEN

Suresh was making his third pilgrimage to Sabarimala. Midway through the forest trail, he twisted his ankle badly. The pain made it impossible to carry his irumudi, and the thought of turning back filled him with sorrow. Just then, a tall man dressed in the pilgrim's black dhoti appeared and asked if he was all right. Before Suresh could answer, the man lifted his irumudi onto his own head and said, 'Let us walk.'

They moved slowly, stopping often. The stranger told stories of past pilgrimages, keeping Suresh's mind off the pain. At one rest point, Suresh realized he had not even asked the man's name. When they finally reached the temple, Suresh turned to thank him, but he was gone.

No one in the group remembered seeing the man enter with them. Suresh offered his prayers with a heart full of wonder, convinced that Lord Ayyappa Himself had walked beside him that day.

Message: In times of weakness, help can come in unexpected forms. Every act of compassion may be a touch of the Divine.

4. THE YOUTH WHO FOUND HIS PURPOSE

Manoj was a restless college student, more interested in late-night parties than discipline or study. When his uncle suggested the Sabarimala pilgrimage, Manoj saw it as a physical challenge, not a spiritual one. The idea of 41 days without meat, alcohol or late nights seemed almost impossible, but he accepted on a dare from friends.

The first week was torture. But as days passed, Manoj noticed changes, his body felt lighter, his mind calmer. The long walks in the evenings with his pilgrim group became times of deep conversation. For the first time, he asked questions about life, God and purpose.

On the final climb to the temple, the sight of thousands of pilgrims chanting in unity struck him with a sudden insight: life is bigger than personal pleasure, and there is joy in contributing to something sacred. That year, Manoj decided to work with an NGO focused on rural education. He says the discipline he learnt during the vrata gave him the strength to commit to a cause larger than himself.

Message: What begins as a challenge can become a turning point when the heart opens to meaning.

5. THE SILENT VOW

Ananthan, a retired army officer, took a vow of silence during his pilgrimage. He wanted to experience the journey without the constant exchange of words, focusing instead on observation and inner reflection.

At first, the silence felt unnatural. He wanted to chat, to share his thoughts about the scenery, to greet people along the way. But as the days passed, his senses became sharper. He noticed the sound of flowing streams, the way the wind moved through the forest, and the sincerity in people's eyes when they nodded to him in greeting.

When he reached the temple, his prayers were wordless. Yet he felt more connected to Ayyappa than in all his previous pilgrimages. The vow of silence had quieted his inner noise, making room for the Lord's presence.

Message: Silence can be a powerful tool for hearing the voice of the Divine.

6. THE FRIEND WHO WAITED

Pradeep and Hari were childhood friends who had planned their first Sabarimala pilgrimage together. On the forest trail, Hari began to feel unwell with fever and fatigue. The group urged Pradeep to go ahead, since stopping would mean missing their planned temple-darshan time. But Pradeep refused. He sat with Hari under a tree, fanning him and giving him water, even though they both knew this meant they would likely miss their slot.

After hours of rest, Hari slowly regained strength and insisted that Pradeep go on without him. Pradeep shook his head and said, 'We started together, we will finish together.' They eventually reached the temple late at night, long after the crowd had thinned. To their surprise, the sanctum was still open for a special *pooja*. The priest looked at them and said, 'You have come at the Lord's time.'

Hari later told others that this pilgrimage was not about reaching the temple quickly, but about realizing that friendship and loyalty are also acts of devotion.

Message: True devotion is not measured in speed or achievement, but in the love and loyalty we show along the way.

7. THE PILGRIM WHO CARRIED NOTHING

Venu was a daily-wage labourer from Kerala. He had dreamt of visiting Sabarimala for years but could never afford the offerings or even a proper irumudi. One year, determined not to miss the chance again, he joined a group with nothing but a small cloth bundle of rice and a bottle of water.

At first, he felt ashamed when he saw others with beautifully packed irumudis and offerings. But along the path, pilgrims shared food, water and sweets with him without hesitation. By the time he reached the temple, he realized that what he carried on his head mattered far less than what he carried in his heart.

Standing before Lord Ayyappa, Venu prayed not for

wealth, but for the grace to have a generous heart always. He returned home with no more money than he had left with, but with a wealth of kindness that he shared with his neighbours daily.

Message: The Lord does not weigh the value of your offering by its price, but by the love with which it is given.

8. THE PILGRIMAGE OF FORGIVENESS

Sankar and his elder brother had not spoken to each other for nearly a decade after a bitter family dispute. That year, both men independently decided to take the Sabarimala pilgrimage, neither knowing the other's plan. On the forest trail, they unexpectedly crossed paths. At first, they avoided eye contact, each carrying the pride of old wounds.

But the trail was long, and eventually they ended up walking beside each other. Without words, one offered water to the other, and the other accepted. Later that evening, at a rest point, they shared a simple meal from the same leaf plate. By the time they reached the temple, the years of silence had dissolved.

At the sanctum, they stood side by side and prayed. Sankar later said, 'It was not I who forgave, nor he who forgave. It was Ayyappa who removed the wall between us.'

Message: Pilgrimage can cleanse more than the body; it can cleanse the heart of years of bitterness.

9. THE YOUNG GIRL WHO CARRIED THE CHANT

Anitha, a 10-year-old from Coimbatore, could not join her father for the forest trek due to school exams. But she made her own vow to chant *Swamiye Sharanam Ayyappa* 108 times each morning and evening until his safe return.

Every day, she lit a small oil lamp at home and sat cross-legged, softly repeating the chant. On the day her father returned, he told her that during the hardest part of the climb, he had felt an unusual calm, as if someone were praying for him. When Anitha told him about her vow, he hugged her and said, 'You walked with me, even from here.'

Message: Devotion is not bound by distance. Sincere prayer bridges any gap.

10. THE PILGRIM WHO SAW AYYAPPA IN EVERYONE

Joseph was a Christian taxi driver in Kochi who often drove groups of Ayyappa devotees to the starting point of their pilgrimage. Over the years, he observed their discipline and unity with quiet admiration. One year, after much encouragement from his passengers, he decided to accompany them for part of the journey, purely out of curiosity.

On the trail, he offered to carry an elderly man's irumudi for a short stretch. Later, he shared his own food with a group who had run out. In every smile and every word of thanks, Joseph began to see a light that felt familiar, the same light he saw in his own church when people helped one another.

When he returned home, Joseph told his wife, 'I may not wear the mala or follow the 41 days, but I have seen what it means to treat every person as if they are God.' He continued driving pilgrims every year, but now with the joy of knowing he was part of their journey in spirit.

Message: The essence of pilgrimage is seeing the Divine in all beings, regardless of religion or background.

PART VI

Equality at Sabarimala, Equality in Life

At Sabarimala, every man is Swamy and every woman near the shrine is honoured as mother or sister within the traditions that govern access and worship. Annadanam, the humble act of feeding pilgrims, cuts through hierarchy. The irumudi makes everyone a carrier. Dust, sweat and song create a democracy of devotion. This is not theoretical equality. It is lived in queues, in shared water, and in the way people step aside for elders and guide children over stones.

1. PRACTICAL HABITS OF EQUALITY

In your team, let juniors speak first in meetings once a week. Tip quietly the people who clean your spaces. Thank them by name. When conflict arises, first restate the other person's concern in your words until they say, 'You got it.'

Then share yours. This equalizes the heart. Invite people from different backgrounds to share their stories in your circle. Practise curiosity without judgment. Celebrate effort, not only results. Build ramps for those who cannot climb stairs. Build listening posts for those who cannot speak loudly.

2. LANGUAGE THAT HEALS DIVIDES

Words can open doors or slam them. Replace 'they' with 'we' whenever you can. Replace blame with responsibility. Replace 'prove' with 'explore'. Replace 'always' and 'never' with 'often' and 'sometimes'. Language shapes reality. Speak as someone who remembers *Tat Tvam Asi*. Speak to the Divine in the other and you will call it forward.

3. LEADERSHIP AS SERVICE

A leader eats last. A leader takes blame and shares credit. A leader turns power into protection for the vulnerable. Sabarimala teaches that the one in front is the one who carries a little more, not the one who demands a little more. Lead like that at school, at work, in your home. Lead like a pilgrim who knows the way and walks beside others, not ahead of them with pride.

PART VII

A 41 Day City Vrata Plan

The **41-day vrata** before Sabarimala is traditionally observed with the discipline of a renunciate, even while living at home. It purifies body, mind and spirit, preparing the devotee to approach Lord Ayyappa with humility and inner strength. For those living in cities today, the same vrata is possible if we adapt without diluting its essence.

Below is a **complete, city-friendly plan** that preserves the original vow's spiritual intent.

CORE PRINCIPLES TO HOLD FOR ALL 41 DAYS

1. **Simplicity in Living**
    - Wear plain, dark-coloured clothes (usually black, blue or saffron) to reduce vanity.
    - Keep personal grooming simple, avoid cosmetics, perfumes and elaborate hairstyles.

2. **Vegetarian Diet and Sattvic Food**

    - No meat, fish, eggs, or intoxicants.
    - Avoid processed junk foods and overeating; focus on home-cooked meals.
    - Eat only when hungry, ideally twice a day.

3. **Celibacy and Purity of Conduct**

    - Maintain mental and physical celibacy to conserve energy.
    - Speak truthfully and avoid gossip or harsh speech.

4. **Daily Worship and Prayer**

    - Set aside fixed times for chanting *Swamiye Sharanam Ayyappa* and reading scriptures.

5. **Selflessness and Service**

    - Perform at least one conscious act of kindness every day without expecting thanks.

DAILY STRUCTURE IN THE CITY

Morning Routine

- **Wake before Sunrise:** Ideally by 4:30 or 5:00 a.m.
- **Personal Cleansing:** Bathe in cold or lukewarm water to awaken the senses.
- **Prayer and Chanting:**
    - Light a lamp.
    - Chant *Swamiye Sharanam Ayyappa* at least 108 times.

    - Read one short passage from the *Bhagavad Gita* or the life story of Lord Ayyappa.
- **Silence Time:** Spend five minutes in quiet meditation on *Tat Tvam Asi*.

Daytime Practice

- At work or school, carry a small mental reminder of your vow: a bead, a photo or simply the chant repeated mentally.
- Practice mindful speech and action: eat with gratitude and listen fully when others speak.
- Avoid excess phone scrolling and unnecessary entertainment.

Evening Routine

- Bathe again after returning home.
- Offer prayers at your home altar or a quiet corner.
- Chant *Swamiye Sharanam Ayyappa* another 108 times.
- Read a spiritual story or reflect on the day's behaviour.
- Sleep early, ideally by 9:30 p.m., to keep the body in balance.

WEEKLY THEMES FOR THE 41 DAYS

Dividing the vrata into **six weekly themes** helps avoid monotony and deepens practice.

1. **Week 1—Simplicity**
    - Declutter your home and desk.
    - Eat the simplest meals possible.
    - Speak only what is necessary and truthful.

2. **Week 2—Self-control**
   - o Avoid impulse buying and unnecessary spending.
   - o Reduce social media to essential communication.
   - o Consciously choose patience in daily situations.
3. **Week 3—Compassion**
   - o Offer help to a colleague, stranger, or neighbour without expecting reward.
   - o Donate something useful to someone in need.
   - o Speak kindly even to those who irritate you.
4. **Week 4—Mindfulness**
   - o Eat every meal slowly and with gratitude.
   - o Practise walking meditation during your commute or break.
   - o Notice your emotional reactions and consciously choose your response.
5. **Week 5—Gratitude**
   - o Each night, write down three things you are grateful for.
   - o Thank at least one person each day sincerely.
   - o Offer prayers for people you have never met.
6. **Week 6—Surrender**
   - o Reflect daily on *Tat Tvam Asi* and the unity of all beings.
   - o Let go of a long-held grudge or hurt.
   - o Trust that everything is unfolding as per the divine plan.

OPTIONAL DEEPER PRACTICES

- **Vrata Journal:** Keep a diary of prayers, reflections and changes you notice in yourself.
- **Weekly Fasting:** Choose one day each week for fruit-and-water fasting, breaking fast after evening prayers.
- **Community *Bhajan*:** Join or host a small chanting session once a week.
- **Charity Offering:** Save a small amount daily to offer at Sabarimala or to a local charity.

FINAL THREE DAYS—HEIGHTENED DISCIPLINE

The last 72 hours before departure are the most intense.

- Speak very little, keep the mind inward-focused.
- Take only simple, light meals.
- Chant more frequently.
- Avoid arguments, distractions or unnecessary travel.
- On the final day before travel, dedicate all actions to Lord Ayyappa.

CHECKLIST FOR A CITY VRATA

✓ Black/blue/saffron clothing ready
✓ Mala or beaded chain to wear for the 41 days
✓ Prayer space set up at home
✓ Daily chanting commitment
✓ Service act planned for each week
✓ Vrata journal
✓ Food plan with vegetarian meals
✓ Travel arrangements for pilgrimage day

A 41-day vrata in the city is not about pretending to be a hermit. It is about creating a **hermit's heart** in the middle of traffic, deadlines and noise. Every time you choose restraint over indulgence, kindness over irritation, or prayer over distraction, you are climbing the first steps towards Ayyappa's presence even before your feet touch Sabarimala soil.

PART VIII

The Dharma Test, a Decision Framework

The life of a devotee is filled with choices. Some are small, like how to respond to a hurtful remark. Other choices are more significant; for example, which career path should one choose, or whether one should stand up against injustice. In a world overflowing with distractions and moral grey zones, we need a compass.

Lord Ayyappa's journey from birth to the vanquishing of Mahishi shows us that a life aligned with dharma is not about following rigid rules but about choosing the action that upholds truth, harmony and the welfare of all.

This section offers a **five-step Dharma Test**. It is a decision-making framework inspired by Ayyappa's life, Vedantic principles like *Tat Tvam Asi,* and the inclusivity of the Sabarimala pilgrimage.

STEP 1: PAUSE AND CREATE INNER SILENCE

Before reacting, stop. Whether you are dealing with a heated conversation or a big life decision, take a conscious pause.

Practical Tip:

- Take three deep breaths before speaking or acting.
- Repeat *Swamiye Sharanam Ayyappa* silently to centre your mind.
- If possible, step away for a moment to gain emotional distance.

Why it matters: Decisions made in haste often come from ego, fear, or desire, not from dharma.

STEP 2: IDENTIFY THE REAL QUESTION

Dharma is not about what is easiest but about what is right. The right question changes everything.

Ask yourself:

- 'What exactly am I deciding here?'
- 'Am I trying to protect my ego, or am I serving a greater good?'
- 'What would this decision look like if I removed my personal benefit?'

Example:

If a friend asks for help with something unethical at work, the real question is not 'Will I help my friend?' but 'Will my help harm others or compromise truth?'

STEP 3: APPLY THE FOUR DHARMA LENSES

Here is where Ayyappa's principles meet modern practicality. Use these four lenses for every important decision.

1. Truth Lens—Is it aligned with Satya (Truth)?

- Is it honest and transparent?
- Would I be comfortable if this decision were made public?

2. Compassion Lens—Does it reduce suffering?

- Will my choice harm anyone unnecessarily?
- Does it uplift, protect, or heal?

3. Duty Lens—Is it in harmony with my svadharma (personal duty)?

- Does it honour my responsibilities to family, work, society, and self?
- Am I neglecting a duty for convenience or pleasure?

4. Oneness Lens—Does it reflect *Tat Tvam Asi*?

- Am I treating others as myself?
- Does it build unity rather than division?

STEP 4: TEST FOR EGO AND DESIRE

The *Bhagavad Gita* teaches that attachment and aversion cloud judgment. Ayyappa's life shows the same truth. He renounced the throne and comforts to fulfil His higher duty.

Ask:

- 'Am I choosing this because it feels good or because it is right?'

- 'If I set aside my personal gain or fear, would I still choose this path?'

Practical Method:

- Imagine you are giving advice to a younger sibling facing this decision. What would you tell them?
- If your decision feels uncomfortable but deeply right, it is probably aligned with dharma.

STEP 5: COMMIT AND ACCEPT CONSEQUENCES

Once the decision is made:

- Act with full commitment. No half measures.
- Accept both success and failure with equanimity.
- Offer the results to the Divine.

Chant mentally: *Tat Tvam Asi*

Everyday Uses of the Dharma Test

The Dharma Test is not just for dramatic life choices. It works for:

- Deciding whether to engage in an argument online.
- Choosing between personal leisure and helping a friend.
- Determining how to respond to unethical behaviour at work.
- Balancing self-care and service to others.

PRACTICAL EXERCISE: THE 21-DAY DHARMA JOURNAL

For 21 days, note one decision you made using the Dharma Test.

Record:

1. The situation.
2. Your thought process using the five steps.
3. The outcome and your feelings afterward.

After 21 days, you will see patterns in how you choose and where ego or fear still influence you.

LESSONS FROM AYYAPPA'S LIFE

1. **Duty above Comfort:** Ayyappa left the comforts of the palace to fulfil the task of ending Mahishi's tyranny.
2. **Compassion with Strength:** He did not seek conflict but acted decisively when needed.
3. **Equality in Action:** He welcomed all devotees, breaking barriers of caste and creed.
4. **Self-mastery:** His life was rooted in discipline, which is the foundation of dharmic living.

The Dharma Test is not about being perfect. It is about training the mind to pause, look beyond the surface, and choose the path that serves truth, compassion and unity. Over time, this process becomes second nature and your life itself becomes a pilgrimage, each choice a step towards the Divine.

PART IX

Working with Five Common Obstacles

No matter how sincere our spiritual journey, obstacles arise. The 41-day vrata, the pilgrimage to Sabarimala, and the application of Ayyappa's teachings in daily life all confront us with challenges. Recognizing these obstacles and learning how to transform them into stepping-stones is part of the path.

In Vedantic thought, obstacles are not enemies. They are opportunities for purification, strength and deeper understanding. Here we explore five common obstacles faced by devotees and modern seekers, along with practical examples and methods to overcome them.

OBSTACLE 1: DISTRACTION

In our times, distraction is perhaps the biggest challenge. Smartphones, streaming platforms, endless notifications: the mind jumps from one stimulus to another.

Example: During your 41-day vrata, you sit down to chant *Swamiye Sharanam Ayyappa*. Five minutes later, you find yourself scrolling through social media, checking messages, and losing the rhythm of your prayer.

How Ayyappa's teaching applies: Ayyappa's journey to Sabarimala was focused and purposeful. He did not allow Himself to be drawn into side quests or temporary pleasures. His discipline shows us that focus is an act of devotion.

Practical Tips:

1. **Device Fasting:** Pick two hours daily to be completely free from devices. Use this time for chanting, reflection or quiet reading.
2. **Micro Practices:** Each time you catch yourself distracted, close your eyes, take three breaths, and repeat the mantra once.
3. **Environmental Cues:** Keep your prayer beads, lamp, or sacred image visible in your main space. Physical reminders bring your mind back to the path.

OBSTACLE 2: DOUBT

Doubt can creep in at different levels. It might be about your capacity, the value of the practice, or even the existence of higher truth.

Example: A week into the vrata, you start questioning: 'Is all this effort really worth it? I am still the same person. Maybe this is just symbolic.'

How Ayyappa's teaching applies: Even when faced with

the immense challenge of confronting Mahishi, Ayyappa held to His mission. His faith in the purpose of His life was unshaken. Faith is not blind belief. It is the courage to keep walking even when the destination is not visible.

Practical Tips:

1. **Return to Stories:** When doubt arises, read one inspiring story from the life of Ayyappa or from past pilgrims.
2. **Buddy System:** Share your journey with a fellow devotee. Talking about your struggles often clears doubts.
3. **Anchor in Experience:** Recall a time when you felt deeply peaceful during prayer. That moment is proof enough for now.

OBSTACLE 3: IMPATIENCE

Many seekers want quick results. We want peace in a week, transformation in a month. Spiritual growth is slower, like a tree maturing over years.

Example: By the fifteenth day of your vrata, you may think, 'Nothing dramatic has happened yet. I still feel stressed at work. Maybe I am doing something wrong.'

How Ayyappa's teaching applies: Ayyappa's own mission unfolded over years, not days. The pilgrimage itself is a long trek through forests and hills, the journey is as important as the destination.

Practical Tips:

1. **Reframe the Goal:** Instead of asking, 'When will I

change?' ask 'Am I walking in the right direction today?'

2. **Daily Gratitude Log:** Note one small blessing from the day. Small changes add up.
3. **Celebrate Milestones:** Mark your seventh, fourteenth and twenty-first days of vrata with a simple offering at home. This builds momentum.

OBSTACLE 4: SOCIAL PRESSURE

Not everyone will understand or support your practices. Some may question why you follow rules like abstaining from certain foods or wearing black or blue attire.

Example: Friends may invite you to a late-night party during your vrata and pressure you to drink or eat meat.

How Ayyappa's teaching applies: Ayyappa welcomed everyone to Sabarimala without judging them, but He also maintained His own vows with clarity. His life reminds us that respect for others does not mean abandoning our principles.

Practical Tips:

1. **Polite but Firm Boundaries:** You do not need to explain in detail, simply say, 'I am on a vrata right now, so I will pass this time.'
2. **Offer Alternatives:** Suggest meeting for a walk or tea instead of a party.
3. **Strengthen Identity:** Wear your mala with awareness. Let it remind you that you are walking a sacred path.

OBSTACLE 5: INNER RESISTANCE

Sometimes the hardest obstacle is not outside but within; laziness, lack of motivation, or old habits pulling us back.

Example: On a rainy morning, you may feel like skipping your prayers and meditation. You tell yourself, 'I will do it tomorrow,' but tomorrow turns into a week.

How Ayyappa's teaching applies: The 41-day vrata is itself a training in overcoming inner resistance. Ayyappa's forest journey involved physical exhaustion, hunger and hardship. Yet He pressed on with purpose.

Practical Tips:

1. **Two-minute Rule:** When resistance appears, commit to just two minutes of practice. Often the mind will want to continue.
2. **Visualize the Goal:** Imagine yourself standing on the eighteenth step at Sabarimala, looking into the sanctum. Let that vision fuel your discipline.
3. **Accountability Partner:** Share your daily goals with someone who will check in with you.

TURNING OBSTACLES INTO ALLIES

The very obstacles that frustrate you can become your greatest teachers. Distraction teaches focus. Doubt deepens faith. Impatience cultivates patience. Social pressure strengthens clarity. Inner resistance builds discipline.

When you face a challenge during your pilgrimage or in everyday life, pause and ask:

- What is this teaching me right now?
- How can this help me grow stronger in my path?

Ayyappa's own life was a sequence of challenges. Each one refined His strength, compassion and wisdom. As modern devotees, we can embrace the same process, knowing that each obstacle, when faced consciously, moves us one step closer to the Divine.

PART X

The Fourfold Daily Reset

The path to Ayyappa is not just about the pilgrimage season. It is about living with awareness every single day. Even the most disciplined devotee will face moments when the mind slips into stress, irritation, or forgetfulness of the Divine. The Fourfold Daily Reset is a way to bring the mind, body and spirit back into alignment at least four times each day.

This practice works like cleaning the windshield of a car during a long journey. Without regular cleaning, dust and splashes block our vision. Similarly, without regular resets, mental noise and emotional clutter block our inner vision.

The Fourfold Daily Reset consists of four deliberate pauses at specific times of the day, each with a different purpose. It can be adapted whether you are on the 41-day vrata, a Sabarimala pilgrimage, or simply living everyday city life.

RESET 1: DAWN—SETTING THE COMPASS

Purpose: Begin the day with direction and intention.

Why it matters: Morning is when the mind is most fresh. If the first thoughts of the day are conscious and elevated, they set the tone for everything that follows. In Vedanta, the first impressions of the day (*pratah samskara*) shape the whole day's mental atmosphere.

Practical Steps:

1. **Wake up Mindfully:** As soon as you wake up, place your palms together and silently say *Swamiye Sharanam Ayyappa* three times.
2. **Water Ritual:** Wash your face with cool water, imagining it washing away any mental dullness.
3. **Sun Greeting:** Stand facing the rising Sun. Close your eyes, take three deep breaths, and visualize the light entering your mind and heart.
4. **One-line Intention:** Decide one quality you want to live today. For example, 'Today I will speak with kindness' or 'Today I will keep my mind steady'.

Modern Example: A young software engineer on the 41-day vrata starts his day at 6:00 a.m., chants for 10 minutes, and writes his one-line intention in a small pocket notebook before leaving for work.

RESET 2: MIDDAY—ENERGY RENEWAL

Purpose: Break the cycle of stress and distraction.

Why it matters: By midday, mental and physical energy

often dip. Without a reset, stress piles up and old patterns take over. In Ayyappa's path, mid-journey rest stops in the forest were essential for pilgrims to recover energy before continuing the trek.

Practical Steps:

1. **Pause and Breathe:** Set a reminder on your phone for a two-minute midday pause.
2. **Mini-mantra Practice:** Close your eyes and repeat *Swamiye Sharanam Ayyappa*' 21 times.
3. **Body Stretch:** Roll your shoulders, rotate your neck, and stretch your spine. This helps release tension.
4. **Gratitude Glance:** Think of one thing that has gone well so far in the day, no matter how small.

Modern Example: A college student on his vrata takes a break at 1:00 p.m. between classes. He sits under a tree, chants for two minutes, and eats a simple lunch in silence before heading back to lectures.

RESET 3: SUNSET—REFLECTION AND OFFERING

Purpose: Transform the events of the day into spiritual learning.

Why it matters: The transition from day to night is a natural point to review, release, and realign. In the pilgrimage, sunset was a time for lighting lamps, offering prayers and resting in gratitude.

Practical Steps:

1. **Light a Lamp:** Even a small tea light can become a sacred focus.

2. **Silent Reflection:** Review the day's events. Ask, 'Where did I act with awareness? Where did I forget?'
3. **Release:** If there were moments of anger, regret or fear, imagine placing them at Ayyappa's feet.
4. **Evening Chant:** End with five minutes of chanting or silent mantra repetition.

Modern Example: A business professional on his vrata returns from work, lights a small lamp in his apartment, chants quietly for a few minutes and writes down one learning from the day.

RESET 4: NIGHT—INNER SURRENDER

Purpose: End the day in peace, ready for rest.

Why it matters: The mind absorbs the last impressions of the day deeply during sleep. If we end the day in frustration or distraction, it carries into the night and the next morning. The final reset ensures we close the day with surrender and faith.

Practical Steps:

1. **Gratitude List:** Write down three things you are thankful for from the day.
2. **Forgiveness Practice:** Silently say, 'I forgive those who hurt me today, and I seek forgiveness from those I may have hurt.'
3. **Mantra Sleep:** Lie down and repeat *Swamiye Sharanam Ayyappa* softly until you drift into sleep.
4. **Visualize the Temple:** Imagine yourself standing on the eighteenth step, seeing the Lord's form, and offering the entire day to Him.

Modern Example: A young father doing his vrata completes his work and household chores, then spends five quiet minutes by his bed doing gratitude journaling and mantra chanting before sleep.

INTEGRATING THE FOURFOLD DAILY RESET INTO MODERN LIFE

- **Start Small:** If four resets feel too much at first, begin with just the dawn and night resets for one week, then add the others.
- **Use Technology Mindfully:** Set reminders for your resets, but do not let them become another source of distraction.
- **Make It Your Own:** Adjust the chanting, reflections, or rituals to match your environment while keeping the spirit intact.

The Fourfold Daily Reset is not about perfection. Some days you may miss one or two resets. That is fine. The goal is to develop the habit of returning to centre repeatedly. Over time, these pauses will become as natural as eating or sleeping.

By consciously resetting four times each day, you keep your inner compass pointing towards the Divine, no matter where you are or what you are doing.

PART XI

The Workplace and Campus Field Guide

For many modern devotees, the workplace or campus is where discipline, faith and values are tested most. You might be dressed in simple black attire, wearing a beaded mala, and keeping your vrata while surrounded by colleagues or classmates who have no idea what that means. You might be juggling project deadlines, meetings and academic assignments while maintaining spiritual discipline.

This guide will help you apply Ayyappa's principles in a busy, modern setting without compromising on the vrata's integrity or your professional and academic responsibilities.

1. CARRY THE PILGRIM MINDSET TO WORK OR STUDY

During the 41-day vrata, you are not just an employee or a student, you are a pilgrim in every environment. That means the office desk, the laboratory, or the classroom becomes part of the journey to Sabarimala.

Practical Application:

- Begin each workday or lecture by mentally bowing to Lord Ayyappa and visualizing the 18 steps.
- If you work in front of a computer, keep a small image of Ayyappa near your monitor or as your phone's wallpaper to remind you of your purpose.

Modern Example: A young software engineer on the 41-day vrata starts his day at 6:00 a.m., chants for 10 minutes, and writes his one-line intention in a small pocket notebook before leaving for work. That intention might be 'Today I will speak with patience' or 'I will not waste my time on gossip'. This sets the tone for the day.

2. PRACTISING RESTRAINT AND SPEECH DISCIPLINE

The workplace and campus are full of opportunities to get drawn into unnecessary arguments, gossip, or negative speech. Ayyappa's vrata includes mind and speech discipline, so consciously choosing words becomes essential.

Practical Tip:

- Avoid reacting immediately to provocations. Pause, take a breath, and respond with calmness.
- Use speech that uplifts, not speech that wounds.
- If colleagues ask about your mala or attire, explain politely and briefly without getting defensive.

3. MANAGING FOOD RESTRICTIONS GRACEFULLY

The vrata involves a strict vegetarian diet and often abstaining from processed or indulgent foods. This can be challenging during office lunches or campus canteen breaks.

Practical Strategies:

- Prepare and carry your own food so you are never pressured into breaking discipline.
- If invited to a meal outside, choose vegetarian options without making a show of it.
- Politely decline alcohol or non-vegetarian items without judging others.

Modern Example:

A college student on the vrata attends a farewell dinner with his classmates at a restaurant. He quietly orders a simple vegetarian meal and spends the evening enjoying the company, without drawing attention to his food choices.

4. BALANCING WORKLOAD AND SPIRITUAL PRACTICE

The demands of work or study can sometimes feel at odds with spiritual discipline, but Ayyappa's teachings emphasize integration, not escape.

Practical Application:

- Schedule your daily chanting, reading or meditation in the early morning and late evening, before and after work or classes.

- Use commute time to listen to Ayyappa bhajans or Vedantic talks instead of idle scrolling on the phone.
- Treat work and study as seva (service), focusing on excellence as an offering to the Divine.

5. MAINTAINING PURITY IN THOUGHT AND ACTION

In a competitive workplace or academic environment, temptation often comes in the form of shortcuts, dishonesty, or bending the truth for personal gain.

Pilgrim Mindset: Ask yourself, 'If this decision was taken in front of Lord Ayyappa, would I still be comfortable making it?' Act in a way that would make you proud to take each step up the 18 golden steps.

6. HANDLING CURIOSITY AND MISUNDERSTANDINGS

Not everyone will understand why you wear black clothes, avoid certain foods or seem quieter than usual. Some may even joke about it.

Practical Tip:

- Respond with kindness, not defensiveness.
- See these moments as opportunities to explain Ayyappa's message of equality and discipline in simple, non-preachy terms.
- Remember that your actions are the best testimony to your faith.

7. AVOIDING EGO IN DISCIPLINE

The 41-day vrata is not about proving your spiritual superiority over others. It is a private offering to the Lord, not a public badge.

Self-check:

- Do not judge colleagues or classmates who live differently.
- Maintain humility and see everyone as a fellow traveller on their own path.

8. MICRO PRACTICES FOR BUSY DAYS

Even on days packed with deadlines, you can stay anchored in your pilgrimage.

FIVE-MINUTE RESET IDEAS:

- Close your eyes and chant *Swamiye Sharanam Ayyappa* silently for 21 repetitions.
- Recall one of the 18 steps and reflect on how you can apply it in the next hour.
- Do one act of kindness without expecting recognition.

9. BUILDING A QUIET CIRCLE OF SUPPORT

Sometimes, fellow devotees at your workplace or campus can offer encouragement and understanding.

Suggestions:

- If possible, have lunch or tea with other devotees during the vrata for moral support.
- Share practical tips, not in a competitive way, but to help one another maintain discipline.

10. SEEING THE WORKPLACE AND CAMPUS AS PILGRIMAGE TRAINING GROUND

Think of every interaction, challenge and task as preparation for climbing the 18 golden steps. In this way, the pressures of modern life do not become obstacles but training exercises for spiritual strength.

FINAL REFLECTION FOR THIS SECTION

Work and study are not separate from devotion. The same patience you use to deal with a difficult boss is the patience you will use while climbing the long trek to Sabarimala. The same humility you practise with a classmate is the humility that will help you bow your head at the sanctum. If you live as a pilgrim in all places, your entire life becomes a sacred journey.

PART XII

Strength with Tenderness, Power with Peace

One of the most striking aspects of Lord Ayyappa's story is that He embodies both the fierce strength of a warrior and the gentle compassion of a saint. On the one hand, He vanquishes the demoness Mahishi and protects the innocent. On the other, He embraces Vavar, a Muslim friend and ally, showing that true power does not fear difference but honours it.

For a modern devotee, especially one living in a world of competition, conflict and constant pressure, this duality, strength with tenderness, power with peace, is the perfect blueprint for living. It teaches us that the highest form of strength is not domination, but self-mastery. The highest form of peace is not passivity, but active, conscious harmony.

1. UNDERSTANDING THE BALANCE

Strength without tenderness becomes harshness. Tenderness without strength becomes weakness. Ayyappa shows that both can exist in perfect balance. His life demonstrates that a true leader, whether in a village or in a corporate boardroom, must carry both a sword and a lotus, the ability to take decisive action when required, and the gentleness to care for others with empathy.

Vedantic Insight:

The *Bhagavad Gita* speaks of the *sthitha prajna*—the one who is steady in wisdom. Such a person acts firmly when action is needed, but remains inwardly undisturbed. This is exactly what Ayyappa represents.

2. STRENGTH WITH TENDERNESS IN DAILY LIFE

Living strength with tenderness means you can be assertive without being aggressive, disciplined without being unkind, and determined without being arrogant.

Practical Applications:

- **In the Workplace:** Handle mistakes firmly but without humiliation. Guide instead of scolding.
- **In Family Life:** Stand by your principles without hurting the feelings of loved ones.
- **In Friendships:** Offer honest feedback, but wrap it in kindness.

Modern Example:

A young project manager is pressured by a client to cut corners. He calmly but firmly refuses, explaining that quality and ethics cannot be compromised. Afterward, he takes time to reassure his team that they did the right thing and thanks them for standing strong.

3. POWER WITH PEACE IN DAILY LIFE

Power is often misunderstood as the ability to control others. True power, as shown by Ayyappa, is the ability to control oneself. Peace is not the absence of conflict, but the presence of inner stability, even when conflict is unavoidable.

Practical Applications:

- **In Leadership:** Make decisions from a place of clarity, not anger or ego.
- **In Public Discourse:** Remain calm even when others speak with hostility.
- **In Personal Growth:** Let challenges be opportunities to deepen your inner stillness rather than react impulsively.

Modern Example:

A university student is publicly criticized by a professor for a minor mistake, but instead of arguing or sulking, he listens respectfully, corrects the error, and later thanks the professor for pointing it out. This disarms the tension and earns quiet respect.

4. THE PILGRIM'S CODE FOR STRENGTH AND PEACE

Ayyappa devotees can adopt a simple 'Strength with Tenderness' code for everyday living:

1. Speak less, listen more. Strength often lies in restraint.
2. Act decisively, but without personal malice.
3. Protect the weak, but without pity, treat them with dignity.
4. Forgive quickly, but do not compromise truth.
5. See differences as opportunities to serve, not reasons to divide.

5. STORIES FROM AYYAPPA'S LIFE

Two episodes from Ayyappa's story capture this balance perfectly:

The Battle with Mahishi:

Mahishi was fierce, dangerous, and a constant threat. Ayyappa's battle with her was swift and decisive. There was no hesitation in confronting evil. Yet, after her defeat, He granted her moksha, liberation from her curse. Strength ended the battle, tenderness offered release.

The Friendship with Vavar:

In a time when religious divisions could easily have caused conflict, Ayyappa honoured Vavar, a Muslim warrior, as a brother and ally. This was not weakness; it was supreme confidence in His own dharma. By honouring Vavar, Ayyappa showed that true power is inclusive and fearless.

6. APPLYING STRENGTH WITH TENDERNESS IN CONFLICT

Whether you are in an office debate, a family disagreement, or a social challenge, this principle can guide you.

Practical Reflection Process:

1. **Pause:** Before speaking or acting, take three slow breaths.
2. **Check Your Motive:** Is your action for the greater good or for ego satisfaction?
3. **Choose Your Tone:** A firm tone without hostility communicates confidence without aggression.
4. **End with Respect:** Even if you disagree, part with dignity and goodwill.

7. MODERN MEDITATIONS ON STRENGTH AND PEACE

At the end of the day, sit quietly and ask yourself:

- Did I act firmly today without hurting unnecessarily?
- Did I offer kindness without letting go of my principles?
- Did I protect my peace even when challenged?

Chant *Swamiye Sharanam Ayyappa* softly while visualizing Ayyappa holding a bow in one hand and offering blessings with the other. Let the bow represent strength, and the blessing hand, tenderness.

8. DAILY-LIFE PRACTICES FOR TODAY'S YOUTH

- **Morning:** Read one teaching from the *Gita* or a short story from Ayyappa's life and reflect on how it applies to your day.
- **During the Day:** When faced with a choice, ask, 'Can I act firmly but kindly here?'
- **Evening:** Journal one example of where you balanced strength and tenderness, and one where you could improve.

FINAL REFLECTION FOR THIS SECTION

Strength without tenderness breeds fear. Tenderness without strength breeds dependence. Ayyappa teaches us to carry both like twin lamps, lighting the way for ourselves and for others. In a modern world of loud opinions and fragile egos, those who master this balance will be pillars of stability, respected for their clarity and loved for their compassion.

To live as Ayyappa lived is to be unshakable in truth, yet gentle in spirit. It is to face the storms of life with the steadiness of a mountain and the softness of rain. When strength is guided by tenderness, and power is anchored in peace, every action becomes a step towards the Divine.

PART XIII

The Inner Temple at Home

When a pilgrim journeys to Sabarimala, he is not simply walking to a physical shrine. He is walking towards the temple that has always existed within himself. The trek through forests and hills is a reflection of the inner journey through the terrain of the mind, with its slopes of joy, valleys of doubt, and rivers of desire.

Creating an **inner temple at home** means building a space and a routine where that same pilgrimage can happen every single day. It is not only about setting up an altar or about lighting a lamp, though those are important. It is also about shaping a way of living in which your home becomes a place where the presence of Ayyappa is felt, where discipline and devotion work together to keep your mind steady, and where every action in your living space becomes an offering.

1. UNDERSTANDING THE CONCEPT OF THE INNER TEMPLE

In Vedanta, the body is seen as the temple, and the heart as the sanctum where the Divine resides. Just as Sabarimala has its 18 sacred steps, our lives have daily steps, habits, choices and thoughts that either lead us towards or away from the presence of God within.

An inner temple at home means:

- **A sacred physical space** that reminds you of the pilgrimage.
- **A sacred daily rhythm** that keeps you connect to your spiritual path.
- **A sacred mindset** that treats every task, from cooking to studying, as worship.

2. SETTING UP A PHYSICAL SACRED SPACE

Choosing the Location:

Pick a quiet corner of your home that can be kept clean and undisturbed. Even if it is only a small table or a shelf, dedicate it fully to your spiritual practice.

Elements to Include:

- A framed image or idol of Lord Ayyappa.
- A simple oil lamp or *diya*.
- A bell to mark the start of prayer.
- A small container of sacred ash or sandal paste.
- A copy of a *stotra* (hymn) or the *Ayyappa Ashtothram* for chanting.

Keeping It Alive:

- Light the lamp daily, ideally at the same time each morning and evening.
- Change flowers regularly if used.
- Wipe the space clean each day as an act of seva (service).

3. DAILY PRACTICES IN THE INNER TEMPLE

Morning:

- Rise before sunrise.
- Wash and wear clean clothes, preferably simple cotton.
- Light the lamp and chant *Swamiye Sharanam Ayyappa* 108 times or recite a chosen *sloka*.
- Sit silently for two to five minutes, focusing on the breath.

Daytime Reminders:

- Keep a small *rudraksha* or *tulsi* mala in your pocket to touch when you need to remember your focus.
- When eating, silently thank Ayyappa for the food before the first bite.
- Use moments of waiting (at traffic lights, in queues) to mentally repeat the mantra.

Evening:

- Offer a short prayer of gratitude for the day.
- Read one story or verse from Ayyappa's life or Vedantic literature.
- Close with three deep breaths, imagining the light of your home altar filling your entire living space.

4. MAKING THE HOME AN ASHRAM

An ashram is not defined by its walls but by the attitude inside them. When creating your inner temple at home:

- **Practise simplicity** by keeping clutter low and avoiding unnecessary noise.
- **Set house rules** that support discipline during the vrata period: no alcohol, no meat, no harsh arguments.
- **Encourage participation** from family members, even if they are not on the same vrata, by inviting them for the evening lamp lighting.

This transforms the home into a living reminder of the pilgrimage, where every corner carries a sense of sanctity.

5. VEDANTIC REFLECTION: *TAT TVAM ASI* AT HOME

The phrase *Tat Tvam Asi* is not meant to be remembered only during temple visits. The inner temple is the place where you practise seeing this truth every day:

- See Ayyappa in each family member, regardless of mood or behaviour.
- Treat household duties as offerings, not chores.
- Remember that your own consciousness is the real sanctum and keeping it pure is the highest form of temple maintenance.

6. CREATING A PILGRIM'S ATMOSPHERE

Pilgrims at Sabarimala feel an immediate shift in atmosphere, the chants, the scent of incense, the sound of bells. You can recreate some of that at home:

- Play Ayyappa bhajans softly in the background during your prayer time.
- Use incense or sandalwood to create a sensory connection to the temple.
- Keep a photo of the Pathinettampadi (the 18 steps) to remind you of the journey.

7. PRACTICAL TIPS FOR CITY DWELLERS

For those living in apartments or busy cities:

- Use noise-cancelling earphones for your meditation if the environment is noisy.
- Keep your altar at eye level so that it catches your attention whenever you pass.
- If lighting a real oil lamp is not possible, use a small LED lamp during travel or at work.

8. THE INNER TEMPLE MINDSET

A clean and inspiring physical space is only the beginning. The true inner temple is mental:

- **Guard your speech:** Avoid gossip and criticism at home.
- **Guard your thoughts:** Refuse to dwell on resentment.
- **Guard your actions:** Treat the home as if Ayyappa Himself lives there.

When this mindset takes root, the whole house feels like a pilgrimage site.

9. DAILY REFLECTION QUESTIONS

At the end of the day, sit by your inner temple and ask:

- Did my words today bring light or darkness into this home?
- Did I treat my family and guests with respect?
- Did I keep my mind on my higher purpose at least once every hour?

10. A SIMPLE RITUAL FOR VISITORS

When a guest enters, welcome them with a small glass of water and a smile. This is not just hospitality but also spiritual discipline, treating every visitor as a representative of the Divine.

FINAL REFLECTION FOR THIS SECTION

When a pilgrim returns from Sabarimala, the mountain remains in his heart. The inner temple at home is a way of keeping the pilgrimage alive year-round. Ayyappa does not need elaborate offerings; He asks for sincerity, discipline, and love. If your home is filled with these, then every room becomes sacred ground, every day becomes a festival, and every act becomes an offering.

The forest path to Sabarimala may be far away, but the steps to your inner temple are always within reach. By keeping it alive, you carry Ayyappa with you, not only for 41 days, but for all the days of your life.

PART XIV

Pilgrim Etiquette for Life

The pilgrimage to Sabarimala is more than a physical journey to a sacred temple. It is a living classroom where lessons in discipline, humility and brotherhood are taught through every step, every chant and every shared meal. For those who truly understand its spirit, the pilgrimage does not end at the 18 steps. The etiquette learned on the path becomes a way of living for the rest of life.

This is what we call **Pilgrim Etiquette for Life**: a set of guiding principles that take the purity of the pilgrimage and weave it into everyday conduct, whether you are in the home, workplace, marketplace or community.

1. THE ESSENCE OF PILGRIM ETIQUETTE

During the 41-day vrata and the trek to Sabarimala, the pilgrim learns:

- To walk in humility, never pushing ahead but moving in harmony with others.

- To speak respectfully and sparingly.
- To be content with simple food and shelter.
- To keep the mind focused on the mantra, *Swamiye Sharanam Ayyappa.*

Pilgrim etiquette for life is simply the art of carrying these habits beyond the pilgrimage season. It is about living as if you are always wearing the mala and walking towards the Lord.

2. KEY PRINCIPLES OF PILGRIM ETIQUETTE FOR LIFE

a. Speak with Restraint

On the pilgrimage, pilgrims avoid unnecessary talk, gossip and argument. In daily life, this becomes the practice of mindful speech, speaking only when it is true, necessary and kind.

b. Share without Attachment

The pilgrim shares food, water and space on the path. In life, this means giving without expecting recognition or repayment. This could be as simple as offering your seat to someone or sharing your lunch at work.

c. Respect All without Distinction

On the pilgrimage, everyone is addressed as Swamy regardless of social or economic status. This can be carried into life by treating every person, from a child to an elder, from a colleague to a stranger, with equal respect.

d. Endure with Patience

Pilgrims stand in long queues for hours without complaint. In life, patience can be practised while waiting in traffic, handling delays at work or dealing with setbacks without losing calm.

3. TRANSLATING PILGRIM CONDUCT INTO DAILY LIFE

On the Road:

When driving or walking in public, maintain the same calm alertness as when walking up the *Sannidhanam* steps. Avoid aggression and remember you are representing Ayyappa's discipline.

At Work:

Keep a balanced mind. Just as a pilgrim accepts whatever weather or terrain comes, accept changes and challenges at work without irritation. Treat each task as an offering.

At Home:

Show the same courtesy to family as you would to fellow pilgrims. Avoid taking loved ones for granted. Keep the home clean and orderly as you would keep your prayer space.

4. PILGRIM'S BODY LANGUAGE

Even without speaking, a pilgrim communicates devotion and discipline through posture, gestures and expressions.

In everyday life:

- Stand and sit with dignity.
- Keep your facial expressions calm and approachable.
- Avoid restless or impatient movements in public.

5. HANDLING CONFLICT WITH PILGRIM GRACE

On the pilgrimage path, disagreements are rare because everyone remembers the higher goal. In daily life, this can be practised by:

- Pausing before reacting to provocation.
- Silently chanting *Swamiye Sharanam Ayyappa* when anger rises.
- Seeking common ground instead of victory in arguments.

6. LIVING IN BROTHERHOOD AND SISTERHOOD

While the pilgrimage has specific restrictions based on tradition, the essence of *Ayyappa Sharanam* is universal brotherhood. Carry this into daily life by:

- Being inclusive and fair in your dealings.
- Offering help to strangers without judgment.
- Joining in community service activities regularly.

7. MAINTAINING THE SIMPLICITY OF A PILGRIM

During the vrata, the pilgrim lives with minimal possessions. After the pilgrimage, while one may return to normal life, it is possible to retain the habit of simplicity:

- Buy only what you need.
- Avoid wastage.

- Be content with basic comforts and avoid craving luxury for its own sake.

8. PILGRIM ETIQUETTE FOR MODERN CHALLENGES

In today's world, distractions are constant and temptations are many. Pilgrim etiquette offers a way to handle them:

- Use technology mindfully. Avoid using your phone in sacred spaces or during meals.
- Keep speech online as respectful as in person.
- Practise restraint in consumption of media and entertainment, choosing content that uplifts.

9. DAILY PILGRIM CHECK-IN

At the end of each day, reflect:

- Did I live with humility today?
- Did I treat everyone equally?
- Did I speak with care?
- Did I remember my higher purpose at least once every hour?

10. THE VEDANTIC CORE OF PILGRIM ETIQUETTE

At its heart, pilgrim etiquette is Vedanta in action. *Tat Tvam Asi* becomes real when you see divinity in the bus conductor, the shopkeeper, the colleague, and the child in the street. When you live with this awareness, every action becomes a form of worship.

The mountain path to Sabarimala may be walked once or twice a year, but the path of pilgrim etiquette can be walked every single day. It keeps the mind humble, the heart open, and the soul aligned with the Divine. When people meet you, they should feel the same peace and respect they feel when meeting a true pilgrim on the sacred path. That is the highest honour for a devotee of Ayyappa.

PART XV

The Youth Oath

SERVING AS A PATH TO ONENESS

In the journey to Sabarimala, seva is not simply a charitable act. It is the very expression of devotion. It transforms the pilgrim from someone seeking blessings into someone who becomes a blessing for others. Every pilgrim who climbs the sacred 18 steps is also expected to serve, whether that is through helping another devotee on the trek, offering water to the thirsty or quietly clearing litter along the path.

Seva in the Ayyappa tradition is both an inner discipline and an outer expression. On the surface, it may look like simple acts of kindness. In truth, it is a training ground for dissolving the ego and recognizing the same divine presence in every person you meet.

THE SPIRIT BEHIND SEVA

When you engage in seva, you are not doing a favour to someone else. You are honouring the God in them. This shift in understanding is essential. The Ayyappa devotee says *Swamiye Sharanam Ayyappa* not only to the deity at the temple but also to the person before him. By serving others, you are bowing to the same consciousness that dwells in you.

In Vedanta, this reflects the core truth of *Tat Tvam Asi*. The giver and the receiver are ultimately one. By serving others selflessly, you are really serving the Self, the Atman.

SEVA DURING THE 41-DAY VRATA

During the vrata period, seva takes many forms:

- Helping an elderly neighbour with errands.
- Cooking *prasadam* for a local bhajan gathering.
- Accompanying fellow devotees to the temple for evening chanting.
- Offering to clean the temple courtyard after a festival.
- Providing food or water to those in need on the way to work.

These are not random acts of kindness, but conscious offerings. Before you begin, silently dedicate the act to Lord Ayyappa. This transforms a mundane task into an act of worship.

THE SABARIMALA SEVA TRADITION

At Sabarimala, seva is everywhere. Volunteers called Annadanam Swamys serve free food to thousands of pilgrims daily. Others work silently at crowd control, cleaning the premises, guiding newcomers, or carrying the bags of the elderly.

One famous story tells of an old pilgrim who collapsed from exhaustion halfway up the hill. A group of young devotees carried him to the temple without saying a word. Later, when asked why they went through such effort, one of them replied, 'We carried Ayyappa Himself'. The heart of seva is to see the Lord in those you serve.

MODERN APPLICATIONS OF SEVA

In the modern city life, seva can happen anywhere. It could be mentoring a junior at work without expecting credit, offering your seat to someone in need, or simply listening to a colleague who is having a difficult day. The form may change, but the spirit remains the same.

Example: A young IT professional on the 41-day vrata decided that his seva would be helping any co-worker struggling with deadlines, even if it meant staying late. By the end of the period, he noticed his own stress levels drop. The act of serving with no personal agenda dissolved his anxiety and deepened his inner peace.

PRACTICAL SEVA PLAN

To make seva a conscious part of your spiritual life, here is a simple plan:

1. **Morning Intention:** Upon waking, decide on at least one act of seva for the day.
2. **Openness to Opportunity:** Stay alert for unexpected chances to serve.

3. **Silent Dedication:** Offer the act mentally to Ayyappa before beginning.
4. **No Expectation:** Do not wait for thanks or recognition.
5. **Night Reflection:** Before bed, recall your act of seva and offer gratitude for being able to serve.

HOW SEVA TRANSFORMS THE HEART

Over time, regular seva purifies the mind. It erodes selfishness and replaces it with compassion. You begin to recognize that the happiness of others is not separate from your own. In the Sabarimala pilgrimage, this awareness is vital, because the ultimate goal is union, i.e. no separation between the Self and other, devotee and Lord.

CLOSING THOUGHT

The joy of seva lies not in the act itself, but in the surrender it brings. You stop asking, 'What will I gain?' and start asking, 'How can I serve?' This shift is the very movement towards God. In serving others, you serve Ayyappa, and in serving Ayyappa, you find yourself.

PART XVI

The Ayyappa Leadership Code

LEADING WITH DHARMA IN A MODERN WORLD

The pilgrimage to Sabarimala is not just a journey to a temple. It is a leadership school in disguise. Every devotee who takes the 41-day vrata is, knowingly or not, training in the art of leading oneself and guiding others. In this way, the Ayyappa tradition provides a timeless code of leadership that is deeply relevant for today's workplaces, communities and even personal life.

LEADERSHIP AS SELF-MASTERY

In the Ayyappa path, leadership begins with mastery over the Self. Before you can guide others, you must discipline your own thoughts, words and actions. The vrata trains you to wake up early, maintain purity of mind, control desires and act with integrity.

If a person cannot keep their own promises to themselves, how can they keep their word to others? This is why in the Ayyappa tradition, the first follower you must lead is yourself.

Practical Tip: During the vrata, keep one daily commitment that is non-negotiable. It could be chanting *Swamiye Sharanam Ayyappa* 108 times every morning or avoiding harsh speech entirely. Over time, your ability to keep commitments strengthens your leadership foundation.

SERVANT LEADERSHIP

In Sabarimala, true leaders are those who serve first. The Guru Swamy who guides a group up the hill is not above the pilgrims. He walks with them, shares in their hardships, and ensures everyone reaches safely. Leadership here is about enabling others to succeed, not seeking personal glory.

Modern Example: A manager at a software company decides to take the Ayyappa leadership approach during a critical project. Instead of pushing deadlines from the top, he spends time understanding the challenges faced by each team member, helps remove obstacles, and even steps in to handle smaller tasks himself. The team delivers ahead of schedule, not out of fear, but because they feel supported.

THE POWER OF EQUALITY

Sabarimala erases markers of status. A CEO and a farmer walk barefoot side by side. All are addressed as Swamy. This environment teaches leaders to see the dignity and potential in everyone, regardless of background.

In modern life, this means treating every team member, client, or customer as equally valuable. Hierarchies may exist for organizational reasons, but respect must remain equal for all.

CLARITY OF PURPOSE

Every pilgrim has one purpose: to have darshan of Lord Ayyappa. This clarity prevents distraction and keeps the group focused through fatigue, weather and hardship. In leadership, having a clear and inspiring vision serves the same function.

Practical Tip: Whether you are leading a project, a community initiative, or your own personal development plan, write down the single sentence that captures your purpose. Keep it where you can see it daily.

DISCIPLINE AND ADAPTABILITY

On the trek, you cannot control the weather, the terrain, or the size of the crowd. You can only control your preparation, mindset and conduct. Leadership requires the same balance of discipline and adaptability. You must stay true to your core values while adjusting to changing circumstances.

LEADING THROUGH EXAMPLE

In the Ayyappa tradition, instructions alone mean little unless the leader lives them. If a Guru Swamy tells others to avoid waste but is careless with prasadam, his credibility vanishes. Modern leadership is no different. Integrity is the unshakable pillar that earns trust.

AYYAPPA'S OWN EXAMPLE

According to tradition, Lord Ayyappa fulfilled His duties with courage and compassion. He protected His kingdom, helped the needy, and upheld dharma even when it required personal sacrifice. His life reminds us that leadership is not about convenience, but about doing what is right.

PRACTICAL DAILY LEADERSHIP PRACTICES INSPIRED BY AYYAPPA

1. **Morning Alignment:** Spend five minutes visualizing the kind of leader you want to be today.
2. **Midday Check-in:** Ask yourself, 'Am I leading through service or through control?'
3. **Evening Reflection:** Identify one decision you made that upheld dharma and one you could improve.
4. **Weekly Seva Leadership:** Once a week, take up a task that benefits others without expectation of return.

CLOSING THOUGHT

The Ayyappa Leadership Code teaches that the highest leader is the highest servant. Leading is not about power over others, but about power with others. When you combine self-mastery, equality, service and clarity of purpose, you become a leader who inspires trust and transforms lives.

PART XVII

Walking the Path in Today's Digital Age

KEEPING AYYAPPA'S SPIRIT ALIVE IN A WORLD OF SCREENS

The world has changed in ways our ancestors could never have imagined. We live in an era where our phones can tell us the weather on the Sabarimala hill in seconds, where online maps guide us to the temple, and where videos of the pilgrimage can be watched from a couch. Yet, with all this technology, the real inner pilgrimage has become more challenging than ever. Distractions are constant. Attention is fractured. The temptation to replace lived experience with digital simulation is always present.

But the teachings of Lord Ayyappa are timeless. They can guide us in the digital age just as powerfully as they did centuries ago. The key is learning how to use technology without becoming a slave to it.

TECHNOLOGY AS A TOOL, NOT A MASTER

A pilgrim's path is defined by discipline. In the digital age, discipline includes controlling how much of your attention you give to screens. Technology should serve your spiritual and life goals, not pull you away from them.

Practical Tip: During your 41-day vrata, set specific times for checking your phone, email or social media. For example, 15 minutes in the morning after prayers and 15 minutes in the evening. Outside these times, keep your phone on silent or away from reach.

DIGITAL MINIMALISM AS MODERN VRATA

The essence of the vrata is to free yourself from unnecessary distractions. Just as you avoid entertainment, luxury food, and indulgent habits during the pilgrimage, you can also practise a digital vrata. This means cutting down on online noise, endless scrolling and unnecessary notifications.

Modern Example: A young marketing professional on the 41-day vrata deletes all non-essential apps from his phone, keeps only work and essential communication tools, and replaces his morning newsfeed habit with chanting and reading a page from a spiritual book. By the end of the 41 days, he feels calmer and more focused.

ONLINE COMMUNITIES FOR GOOD

While technology can distract, it can also connect. Ayyappa devotees around the world share prayers, guidance and support through online groups. Used wisely, these spaces can help you stay motivated and accountable during the vrata.

Practical Tip: Join a small, disciplined WhatsApp or Telegram group of fellow devotees. Share your daily *sadhana*, small reflections and challenges. The group should have clear rules to prevent it from turning into idle chatter.

MINDFUL CONTENT CONSUMPTION

What you feed your mind is as important as what you feed your body. During the vrata, avoid movies, songs and shows that stir unnecessary desire or restlessness. In the digital age, this also means avoiding content that provokes anger, envy or negativity.

Practice: Before clicking on a video or reading an article, ask yourself, 'Will this help me grow in devotion, wisdom or peace?' If the answer is no, skip it.

HARNESSING DIGITAL FOR DHARMA

The same phone that can waste hours can also be your temple bell, scripture library and meditation guide. There are apps for chanting mantras, tracking daily sadhana, and reading holy texts. The difference lies in intention and discipline.

Practical Tip: Create a 'spiritual folder' on your phone with apps for chanting, reading scriptures, and tracking your vrata progress. Keep it on your home screen and make it your first go-to when you unlock your phone.

DIGITAL DETOX PILGRIMAGE DAYS

Pick one day during the 41-day vrata when you completely avoid non-essential technology. Spend that day in offline devotion, reading scriptures, walking in nature, serving others or meditating. This small act can refresh the mind and deepen your practice.

SOCIAL MEDIA HUMILITY

During the pilgrimage, humility is as important as devotion. In the digital age, it is easy to post photos of every moment of your journey. But the deeper value lies in living the experience rather than broadcasting it for approval.

Reflection: Before posting about your vrata or pilgrimage, ask yourself if you are sharing to inspire others or to seek praise. If it is for the latter, consider keeping it private as a sacred offering to the Lord.

THE VIRTUAL DARSHAN TRAP

Live streams and virtual tours are useful for those who cannot physically make the trip. But they are not replacements for the real experience. Walking barefoot on the forest path, enduring the physical challenge and chanting with fellow pilgrims creates a transformation that a screen cannot replicate.

DAILY DIGITAL GROUNDING

The modern pilgrim must learn to ground themselves amidst constant information overload. Set a daily grounding ritual where you disconnect from all devices and spend at least 20 minutes in stillness, prayer or chanting.

CLOSING THOUGHT

The digital age presents both challenges and opportunities for the Ayyappa devotee. The path is the same as it has always been: discipline, humility and devotion. But now, the pilgrimage includes not only the physical journey to Sabarimala but also the inner journey of mastering your attention in a world designed to steal it. When you use technology as a servant of your spiritual growth, it becomes a powerful ally. When you let it lead you, it becomes the greatest obstacle.

PART XVIII

Q&A for Tough Moments

Q1: I am on the 41-day vrata, but my friends keep inviting me to parties and social gatherings. I feel left out. What should I do?

Answer: The feeling of being left out is natural, but remember that the vrata is a conscious choice to step away from certain pleasures for a higher purpose. Politely explain to your friends that you are observing a discipline and cannot attend events that may conflict with it. Instead, offer to meet them for a simple walk or tea. Over time, many will respect your commitment, and you might inspire someone to take a similar path.

Practice Tip: Keep a list of short, meaningful activities that align with your vrata discipline, such as visiting a temple, reading a few verses from the scriptures or doing seva. Use these as alternatives when the temptation to join social events grows strong.

Q2: I live in a joint family, and not everyone supports my vrata practices. How do I handle criticism or teasing?

Answer: Lord Ayyappa Himself faced challenges and opposition during His life. The key is to practise patience and humility. Avoid arguments and do not try to force your discipline on others. Instead, quietly live your practice with sincerity. Often, silent consistency speaks louder than words.

Practice Tip: Begin your day by praying for the well-being of your family members, including those who do not understand your path. This softens your heart and prevents resentment from building up.

Q3: I am finding it hard to wake up early for prayers. The body feels heavy and the mind just wants more sleep.

Answer: This is a common obstacle, especially in the first week of the vrata. Remind yourself that each early morning you win over sleep, you strengthen your willpower. Try going to bed earlier, keeping your phone away from your bed, and preparing your prayer space the night before.

Practice Tip: Place a small picture of Lord Ayyappa or your *ishta devata* where you will see it first thing in the morning. The visual reminder can help you rise with devotion rather than reluctance.

Q4: I feel spiritually dry. Even though I am doing the rituals, I do not feel inspired.

Answer: Spiritual dryness happens when actions lose connection to intention. Go back to the reason you started the vrata. Read the story of Lord Ayyappa, listen to bhajans, or talk to an elder pilgrim. Inspiration often returns when you reconnect with the heart of the practice.

Practice Tip: Keep a daily gratitude journal during your vrata. Write down one blessing you have noticed that day, no matter how small. Gratitude awakens devotion.

Q5: I slipped. I ate something I should not have during the vrata. Does this mean my vrata is broken?

Answer: One slip does not erase sincere effort. The vrata is about transformation, not perfection. Recognize the mistake, reflect on why it happened, and return to your discipline with more awareness. Do not let guilt paralyse you.

Practice Tip: If you slip, add a small act of devotion that day, such as extra chanting or helping someone in need. Let the error become a stepping stone rather than a stumbling block.

Q6: I face constant negativity at work or college, and it makes it hard to maintain peace.

Answer: You cannot always control your environment, but you can choose your inner state. Think of your mind as a temple and protect it from unhelpful thoughts. Practise detachment and keep your focus on your duties without being drawn into unnecessary conflicts.

Practice Tip: Between tasks, pause for 30 seconds, close your eyes, and silently chant *Swamiye Sharanam Ayyappa*. Even brief resets can protect your inner calm in a noisy environment.

Q7: People question why I am taking this path at my age, saying I am missing out on fun.

Answer: True fun is peace of mind and the joy of purpose. The pilgrimage is a training for life, not an escape from it. You are not missing out; you are gaining a discipline that will serve you far beyond these 41 days.

Practice Tip: Whenever doubts arise from others' comments, mentally repeat the purpose of your vrata. This strengthens resolve and clears confusion.

Q8: I want to continue my discipline after the pilgrimage, but I am afraid I will lose momentum.

Answer: The end of the pilgrimage is not the end of the journey. Carry one or two key practices into your daily life, such as early morning prayer or avoiding certain distractions. Small habits maintained consistently will keep the flame alive.

Practice Tip: Set a reminder for yourself on the day you return from Sabarimala. Mark it as 'Renew My Commitment'. This keeps the transition intentional rather than accidental.

Q9: I feel proud of my discipline and devotion. But is this pride wrong?

Answer: Pride in the sense of gratitude for being able to serve the Lord is good. But pride that makes you feel superior to others can weaken your spiritual progress. Always remember that the strength to complete the vrata comes from divine grace, not personal greatness.

Practice Tip: Whenever you feel pride rising, offer that feeling back to Lord Ayyappa as a prayer of thanks.

Q10: I am overwhelmed by how many rules there are. How do I keep from feeling trapped?

Answer: The rules are not meant to trap you but to free you from the grip of habits that cloud your inner vision. Look at them not as restrictions, but as tools for clarity. Start by focusing on a few key disciplines and build from there.

Practice Tip: List the top three disciplines that have the most positive effect on your mind and body. Keep your attention on these, while gradually improving in others.

CLOSING REFLECTION

Tough moments are part of every spiritual path. They are not signs of failure but invitations to deepen your practice. Lord Ayyappa's life shows that courage, discipline, and compassion can turn even the hardest trials into opportunities for growth. Keep asking the right questions, and the answers will keep you on the path.

PART XIX

The Return Journey and Carrying Sabarimala Home

MAKING THE PILGRIMAGE A LIFELONG COMPANION

The journey to Sabarimala is not complete when you step out of the temple and walk down the sacred steps. In truth, that is where the deeper journey begins. The 41 days of discipline, the climb to the temple, the darshan of Lord Ayyappa, all of these are like intense training for the heart and mind. Once you return to daily life, the challenge is to preserve the fragrance of that experience.

Many pilgrims feel a strange emptiness after the pilgrimage. The structured days, the constant chanting, the shared devotion, all seem to dissolve in the noise of the city or village. This is why it is important to carry Sabarimala home in a real and practical way.

1. THE INNER RETURN: WHAT YOU BRING BACK

When you carry your irumudi and climb the 18 steps, you are leaving behind old patterns and opening to a new way of being. That transformation does not vanish when you remove your mala at the end of the pilgrimage. It becomes part of you. What you bring back is not just memories but new eyes to see the world. You return with:

- A sharper awareness of your own mind.
- A deeper patience with people.
- A new respect for discipline.
- A stronger sense of connection with the divine.

2. CREATING A GENTLE LANDING

Returning from the pilgrimage can feel like waking from a dream. If you rush back into every old habit, the peace you gained will fade quickly. Plan for a gentle re-entry into your routine.

- Keep waking up early for at least the first week after your return.
- Continue your morning chant or prayer for at least 15 minutes daily.
- Avoid overloading your schedule in the first few days. Give yourself time to absorb the experience.

3. KEEPING THE KEY PRACTICES ALIVE

Out of all the practices you followed during the vrata, choose a few that you will continue for the long term. This can include:

- A fixed morning prayer time.
- Avoiding certain distractions that weaken your focus.
- Keeping a gratitude diary.
- Setting aside one day a month for a personal mini-vrata, where you reduce social activities and focus on sadhana.

4. EXTENDING SEVA BEYOND THE PILGRIMAGE

Seva does not end when you return home. If you have been helping other pilgrims or serving at the temple, find ways to serve in your local community. This could be:

- Helping at a local temple or bhajan group.
- Supporting a young pilgrim who is taking the journey for the first time.
- Organizing a small prayer gathering at home.

Seva keeps your heart open and your devotion active.

5. THE YEAR-ROUND PILGRIM MINDSET

Being a pilgrim is not about the clothes or the mala, it is about the mind you carry. You can live with the same awareness all year by:

- Approaching work as a form of worship.
- Treating every person you meet with respect.
- Keeping your speech clean and your thoughts honest.

Remembering that every challenge is part of the path.

6. SHARING THE LIGHT WITHOUT PREACHING

The most powerful way to share the spirit of Sabarimala is by living it. When people notice your calm, discipline, and kindness, they may ask about your path. Share your experiences honestly, but without trying to impose them. True inspiration is silent and gentle.

7. SETTING A DATE FOR THE NEXT PILGRIMAGE

Mark the date for your next pilgrimage soon after you return. This gives you a goal to look forward to and a reason to keep your practices alive. Use the months in between as preparation, not as a break. This way, each year's journey builds on the last.

8. OVERCOMING THE POST-PILGRIMAGE DIP

It is common to feel a dip in energy or mood after returning. This is the mind adjusting to a less intense spiritual atmosphere. You can overcome it by:

- Staying in touch with fellow pilgrims.
- Listening to Ayyappa bhajans.
- Revisiting your pilgrimage diary or photo album.
- Attending local temple events that rekindle the spirit.

CLOSING REFLECTION

Sabarimala is not a place you visit once a year. It is a spiritual state that you can carry in your heart every day. The patience you learnt while waiting in the queue, the humility you felt while walking barefoot, the devotion you experienced in the temple, all of these are seeds that can grow anywhere. The real pilgrimage begins when you return and choose to live as if every step you take is on the sacred path. In this way, you never really leave Sabarimala. You carry it with you, and it shapes your life in quiet, powerful ways.

PART XX

Closing Thoughts and Call to Action

CARRYING THE SPIRIT OF SABARIMALA INTO EVERYDAY LIFE

As we reach the conclusion of this journey, it is essential to remember that Sabarimala is more than a temple, more than a pilgrimage. It is a guide for life, a framework that helps the modern individual navigate challenges with courage, discipline and devotion. The 18 steps, the 41-day vrata, the lessons of seva, and the inner practices are all designed not just for ritual but also for transformation.

1. THE PATH IS CONTINUOUS

The pilgrimage shows us that spiritual growth is continuous. Life presents daily tests, small and large, and each moment is an opportunity to apply what we have learnt. The steps at Sabarimala are mirrored in our lives: each decision, each act of patience, each moment of integrity is a step towards higher consciousness.

It is easy to return to old habits, to forget the clarity and focus of the pilgrimage. The call to action is to remain vigilant, to practise self-awareness and reflection every day. The journey is never truly over.

2. INTEGRATING *TAT TVAM ASI* INTO MODERN LIFE

The Vedantic teaching of *Tat Tvam Asi* is not abstract philosophy. It is a practical guide for everyday living:

- When you face anger or frustration at work, remind yourself of the underlying oneness in all beings.
- When ambition tempts you to cut corners, remember that your higher Self is aligned with dharma, not shortcuts.
- When you encounter suffering, understand that empathy and service are expressions of your true nature.

This teaching encourages humility, responsibility and compassion while keeping the modern individual grounded in real-world action.

3. LIVING THE 18 STEPS DAILY

Each of the 18 steps holds timeless wisdom. Carry them into your routines.

These steps are not just spiritual ideals but practical tools. Living them daily gradually transforms habits, decisions and relationships.

4. MAKING DEVOTION PRACTICAL

Devotion does not require grand gestures. It is expressed in:

- Being present in every conversation.
- Offering help without expecting return.
- Maintaining calm in stressful situations.
- Observing ethical principles consistently.
- Reflecting on the Divine in ordinary life.

By seeing each act as an offering, you bring the energy of Sabarimala into every aspect of existence.

5. THE ROLE OF SEVA

The joy of serving others cannot be overstated. Service is both a test and a blessing. The act of helping without expectation dissolves ego, strengthens empathy, and connects you to the larger world. Even small acts like helping a colleague, supporting a community initiative, or mentoring a student can be sacred when performed with awareness and sincerity.

6. OVERCOMING CHALLENGES

Life will challenge your commitment. Distractions, societal pressure and personal difficulties may try to pull you away from your spiritual path. The lessons of the pilgrimage provide tools to face these:

- Pause and reflect before reacting.
- Revisit your personal vows or practices.
- Engage in meditation or prayer to centre yourself.

- Seek guidance from those who walk the path with integrity.

These are not weaknesses to avoid but opportunities to strengthen resolve and deepen understanding.

7. BUILDING A COMMUNITY

Spiritual growth thrives in supportive environments. Connect with like-minded individuals. Share experiences, support each other in challenges, and celebrate progress together. This mirrors the pilgrim community at Sabarimala where caste, status and background dissolve, leaving only devotion and respect.

8. A CALL TO THE YOUTH

For today's youth, Sabarimala offers an invaluable template for life:

- Discipline builds freedom.
- Self-control fosters clarity.
- Reflection encourages resilience.
- Devotion nurtures purpose.
- Service develops leadership with compassion.

You are not being asked to renounce the modern world but to navigate it with awareness, integrity and courage. The pilgrimage teaches that the real power is subtle, internal, and available to anyone willing to commit to the path.

9. CARRYING SABARIMALA HOME

In practical terms, carrying Sabarimala home means:

- Maintaining a daily ritual or practice, even if brief.
- Applying the 18 steps to real-world decisions.
- Serving others consistently and selflessly.
- Reflecting regularly on your thoughts, words and actions.
- Living in a way that balances ambition with ethics, action with awareness, and strength with tenderness.

The temple is not a building; it is a state of mind. Your life can become a living shrine when you embody the principles learnt on the pilgrimage.

10. CLOSING REFLECTION

As you close this book, remember that Sabarimala is not a destination but a journey of transformation. Every effort you make to integrate its teachings is a step closer to self-mastery and alignment with the Divine.

You are called not to mimic rituals but to embody their essence. You are invited to live fully, ethically and consciously. You are encouraged to take the wisdom of the 18 steps, the 41-day vrata, and the inner practices and make them a practical compass for life.

In carrying Sabarimala into your daily life, you become a beacon of hope, compassion and strength for yourself and for the world around you.

Your journey continues, step by step, moment by moment, until every action becomes an offering, and every day reflects the light of Lord Ayyappa within you.

Practical Toolkits and Checklists

FOR A MODERN PRACTITIONER

Practical tools help turn spiritual insights into daily action. Each toolkit below is designed to be easy to follow, highly applicable, and suitable for modern youth while staying rooted in the spirit of Sabarimala.

1. FIVE-MINUTE RESET FOR STRESS

This short routine can be used anytime during the day to regain calm, clarity, and focus.

Breath Box

- Inhale for four counts, hold for four counts, exhale for four counts, hold for four counts.
- Repeat for four to six cycles. This regulates the nervous system and helps manage anxiety.

Body Scan

- Close your eyes and bring attention to your body. Relax the jaw, shoulders and belly.
- Slowly move attention from head to toe, releasing tension as you notice it.

Focus

- Name one task you will do next. Keep it simple.
- Visualize completing it successfully. This trains your mind to stay present.

Kindness

- Mentally send one blessing to someone you care about or someone you encountered today.
- This cultivates compassion and reduces negative thinking.

Move

- Stand up, stretch arms overhead, rotate shoulders and move your neck gently.
- Even small movements refresh blood circulation and clear mental fog.

Practical Tip: Use this reset before meetings, study sessions or whenever stress builds. Keeping it under five minutes makes it accessible and easy to integrate.

2. WEEKEND RENEWAL PLAN

Weekends are an opportunity to recharge and align yourself with the values of devotion, service and reflection.

Half a Day in Nature

- Go for a walk, hike, or sit by a river, lake or garden. Leave your phone aside.
- Observe your surroundings fully, breathing deeply and noticing small details.

Two Hours of Service

- Volunteer in a local community project, help a neighbour, or support a friend in need.
- Service connects you to a purpose beyond yourself and cultivates humility.

Two Hours of Learning

- Read, watch educational content or practise a skill.
- Focus on learning without distraction, noting insights in a journal.

One Hour of Silence

- Spend an hour without talking, scrolling or screen time.
- Meditate, reflect or simply observe thoughts. Silence strengthens self-awareness.

One Hour of Playful Movement

- Dance, play a sport, or do yoga. Move for joy, not just for exercise.
- Physical play refreshes energy and creativity.

Practical Tip: Plan these activities in advance. Treat the weekend as sacred space to reset mind, body and spirit.

3. STUDY COMPANION

This toolkit helps maintain focus, balance and gratitude during study or work sessions.

Pomodoro Flow

- Set a timer for 25 minutes. Work on one task with full attention.
- Take a five-minute break, stretch or drink water.
- Repeat four cycles.

Longer Break

- After four cycles, take a longer break of 15 to 30 minutes. Walk, hydrate or relax.

Gratitude End

- At the end of your session, write a short note of gratitude to someone who supported your learning.
- Acknowledge teachers, peers or family. Gratitude builds resilience and focus.

Practical Tip: Use this method daily for study, project work or creative pursuits. Consistency is more valuable than duration.

4. RELATIONSHIP FIRST AID

Conflicts and misunderstandings are inevitable. These steps help repair and strengthen relationships.

Do No Harm in Speech

- Pause before reacting. Speak calmly, avoiding blame or judgment.

Acknowledge the Other Person's Story

- Listen actively. Repeat back what you heard to ensure understanding.

State Your Need Clearly

- Use simple, honest statements about what you want or need.

Propose One Small Next Step

- Suggest a small, achievable action that moves the relationship forward.

Agree to Review

- Decide on a time to check progress or revisit the discussion if needed.

Practical Tip: Keep interactions brief and focused during conflicts. Avoid over-explaining or justifying.

5. VALUES TO LIVE BY

These guiding principles help make daily choices aligned with the spirit of Ayyappa and Sabarimala.

Simplicity over Show

- Choose experiences and possessions that add meaning, not just status.

Service over Status

- Measure impact by contribution, not recognition.

Truth over Comfort

- Speak and act honestly, even when it is uncomfortable.

Learning over Looking Right

- Prioritize curiosity and growth over proving yourself correct.

Compassion over Convenience

- Act kindly, even when easier options exist.

Oneness over Winning Alone

- Seek collaboration, unity and collective well-being instead of personal gain only.

Practical Tip: Review these values weekly. Note where you acted in alignment or drifted away. Gradual reinforcement transforms them from concepts into habits.

CLOSING REFLECTION

These toolkits and checklists are designed for immediate application. Using them regularly creates a life that blends modern responsibilities with ancient wisdom. They allow youth to carry the principles of Sabarimala, the discipline of the 18 steps, and the inner teachings of Ayyappa into every moment of work, study, relationships and self-reflection.

By practising daily resets, weekend renewals, mindful study, relationship repair, and living core values, you develop resilience, compassion, clarity and a strong connection to your inner temple. These are practical ways to embody devotion and purpose in a modern, fast-paced life.

The Message to Carry Everywhere

Sabarimala is not just a sacred hill. It is a way of walking on any street, moving through life with awareness and integrity. The 18 steps are not merely a staircase to the shrine. They are 18 ways of being that teach patience, courage, humility and clarity. They guide you to become steady in purpose, useful to others, and free in spirit. Each step represents a lesson that can be applied at home, at work, or among friends. They are lessons in balance, showing how power and tenderness, ambition and compassion, discipline and joy can exist together.

The life of Swamy Ayyappa demonstrates that courage and tenderness can inhabit the same heart. He shows that strength is not only physical or visible, but also moral, emotional and spiritual. His example encourages facing challenges without fear, while acting with kindness towards all beings. Vedanta teaches that the same light burns in every person. Recognizing this unity helps dissolve artificial boundaries of caste, status, religion or language. Equality is not a concept to debate. It is a practice to live every day, in every interaction.

For the youth of today, this message is especially powerful. Modern life demands skill, speed and innovation, yet it also tests patience, focus and character. Sabarimala's lessons bridge both worlds. Coding and compassion can coexist. Ambition and integrity can walk hand in hand. Discipline can protect joy, and devotion can power excellence. You do not need to choose between spiritual life and worldly success. Living as a pilgrim integrates them naturally.

In practical terms, carrying this message involves small, consistent acts. When you forget your principles, begin again without judgment. When you fall, rise gently and reflect on what the experience teaches. When you succeed, share the credit and celebrate the effort of others. When you meet another person, pause and remember *Tat Tvam Asi*. Recognize the same light and potential in them that exists within yourself. When loneliness arises, chant *Swamiye Sharanam Ayyappa*. Listen carefully for the quiet strength that answers from your own chest. That is your inner guide, always present.

Every action can be sacred if approached with attention and care. Eating mindfully, speaking truthfully, listening fully, working with purpose, resting consciously and serving others all become pilgrim practices. Let these everyday rituals become your 18 steps in miniature. The staircase of Sabarimala becomes a mirror for the staircase of life. The discipline, courage and devotion learnt on the hill can be embodied on the street, in your home, in classrooms, offices or studios.

May these steps become your steps. May this path become your path. May your life become a temple of truth and love, and every gesture blessed by God. May your mind be clear, your heart open, and your spirit unwavering. Carry this message in your thoughts, in your words and in your actions. Let it guide the choices you make, the challenges you face, and the opportunities you embrace.

Remember, a life lived as a pilgrim does not separate the sacred from the ordinary. Every moment becomes an opportunity to practise patience, courage, kindness and unity. Every day, you can climb the 18 steps within yourself, reaching a higher understanding, a stronger character and a deeper connection to the world and to God. Let Sabarimala's teachings flow through your life, shaping not just your deeds but your character, your mind and your heart as well.

In all things, walk steadily, act wisely, love generously and serve faithfully. These steps are not just for a hilltop. They are for every street, every home and every heart. They are for you, for the youth of today, and for the generations to come. Carry them everywhere and watch how your life transforms into a living temple of truth, joy, and divine presence.

APPENDIX

Quick Reference Cards

These cards are designed to be carried in your mind, pocket or desk. Each card represents a small, actionable practice that helps integrate the lessons of Sabarimala and Swamy Ayyappa into daily life. They are simple, repeatable and can be adapted to any environment. Use them as reminders to pause, reflect and act with awareness.

CARD A: MORNING STARTER

Begin your day with intention and clarity.

1. Light a lamp or incense, or sit by a window with natural light to mark the start of your practice. Let this physical gesture remind you that today is a sacred opportunity.
2. Take three slow, deep breaths. Inhale fully, pause, exhale completely, and rest for a moment. Let each breath connect you to the present moment.
3. Speak or write one line of prayer. This can be a

traditional mantra, a personal invocation or simply a statement of gratitude.

4. Write or say one line of intention for the day. For example: 'Today I will be helpful to others,' or 'Today I will act with honesty and courage.'
5. Identify one practical kindness you will perform before noon. It can be as simple as helping a colleague, sending a thoughtful message or offering assistance to someone in need.
6. Reflect for one minute on how your actions can align with the principles of courage, compassion and discipline.

Tip: Keep a small notebook or sticky note to track intentions and kindnesses. This builds consistency and reinforces your awareness throughout the day.

CARD B: MIDDAY RESET

Pause during the busyness of the day to restore balance.

1. Drink a glass of water with full awareness. Notice the taste, temperature and sensation. Treat this as a moment of gratitude for the nourishment.
2. Reaffirm your main task for the day. Ask yourself: 'Am I moving with focus and purpose? What needs my attention most right now?'
3. Send a quick thank you message to someone who has helped or inspired you that day. Gratitude strengthens relationships and uplifts your own heart.

4. Take two minutes of silence. Close your eyes, release tension from your body, and allow your mind to rest. Observe any thoughts without judgment.
5. Optionally, stretch your shoulders, arms or legs for one to two minutes. Gentle movement clears energy and refocuses attention.

Tip: Set a reminder on your phone or calendar for this reset. Even a short pause can prevent you from being overwhelmed and improve clarity for the rest of the day.

CARD C: EVENING CLOSURE

Wind down and reflect to complete your daily practice.

1. Note one learning from the day and one thing for which you are grateful. Writing it down solidifies awareness and encourages reflection.
2. Offer your mistakes and lapses to God, Swamy Ayyappa or the higher ideal you follow. This cultivates humility and reduces self-criticism.
3. Read one paragraph from a sacred text, spiritual guide or inspirational reading. Focus on the meaning rather than speed.
4. Take a few deep breaths, relax your body and consciously release the tensions of the day.
5. Prepare for sleep with the intention of rest, renewal and openness for tomorrow.

Tip: Keep a bedside notebook or journal. Tracking your reflections nightly helps you see patterns of growth and areas for continued practice.

CARD D: CONFLICT MOMENT

Use this card when faced with disagreement, anger or tension.

1. Pause immediately. Even a few seconds of conscious breathing can prevent escalation.
2. Identify the need or feeling behind your anger. Naming it clearly reduces unconscious reactivity. For example, 'I feel overlooked' or 'I need clarity'.
3. Acknowledge the other person's need. This creates empathy and prevents judgment.
4. Propose one small, respectful next step. For example, suggesting a short conversation, a compromise or a break to cool off.
5. Mentally or verbally, bless the outcome. Accept that the resolution may not be perfect, but the intention is to act with awareness and integrity.

Tip: Practise this card even in minor disagreements. Over time, responding with awareness becomes natural and strengthens relationships.

CARD E: STUDY SPRINT

Enhance focus and learning with structured short bursts of practice.

1. Set a timer for 25 minutes and work on a single task or subject with full attention. Avoid multitasking.
2. After the sprint, take five minutes to stand, stretch and hydrate. Physical reset supports mental clarity.

3. Repeat this cycle three times. Observe your energy, focus and progress during each sprint.
4. After completing the cycles, reward yourself with a short walk, some fresh air or a moment of quiet reflection.
5. End with a gratitude note, either mentally or written, acknowledging anyone who supported your study, inspiration or environment.

Tip: Combine this with intention setting. Begin each study sprint with a simple phrase such as, 'I will focus and learn with attention and humility.'

These quick reference cards serve as mini-pilgrimages for daily life. Each one distils the principles of Sabarimala and Swamy Ayyappa into actionable steps. Carry them in your mind, adapt them to your schedule, and return to them often. Consistent use nurtures focus, discipline, courage, compassion and joy, creating small temples of practice wherever you go.

EPILOGUE

The Path that Walks with You

Sabarimala is more than a hill. It is a mirror of life itself. The 18 steps are more than stones. They are 18 ways of being that shape courage, discipline, compassion and wisdom. Each step invites you to look inward, to confront your fears, to act with integrity and to rise stronger. Swamy Ayyappa's life shows that power can be gentle, courage can be tender, and devotion can be practical.

The light of Vedanta reminds us that the same spark that shines in the saint shines in you and in every other being. *Tat Tvam Asi* is not just a phrase to memorize. It is a way of seeing the world through the eyes of unity. When you meet another person, when you face difficulty, when your ambition drives you forward, remember that you are not separate. You are part of the same whole. Your choices echo beyond yourself. Your actions shape more than your day.

The youth of today have the rare opportunity to live with the best of both worlds. You can simultaneously code with curiosity and care. You can compete with excellence and act with ethics. You can succeed in the material world while nurturing your inner temple. Discipline becomes a shield, reflection becomes a compass, service becomes joy, and devotion becomes strength.

Walk your streets, your campuses, your workplaces as a pilgrim. Let the 18 steps guide your actions. Begin again when you falter. Rise gently when you fall. Share credit when you win. Speak truth with courage. Listen with empathy. Every challenge becomes a lesson. Every encounter becomes a chance to practise equality, patience and love.

When fear comes, breathe. When doubt comes, remember your intention. When loneliness comes, whisper *Swamiye Sharanam Ayyappa* and feel the quiet strength that rises in your own chest. Let the practices, the reflections and the tools you have learnt be companions on your journey. They are not rules to follow, but rather invitations to live fully and with purpose.

May these teachings not remain on a page. May they become your steps, your habits, your decisions, your prayers, and your work. May your life become a living temple where truth is honoured, love flows freely, courage meets tenderness, and God resides in every heartbeat. The path is not easy, yet it is simple. The path is not distant, yet it is profound. Step forward with intention, step forward with humility, step forward with joy. The pilgrimage does not end at Sabarimala. It continues in every act, every word and every thought of your life. Carry the steps, carry the light, carry the love. Let your life be the answer the world has been waiting for.

Acknowledgements

My heartfelt gratitude begins with the divine. With folded hands, I offer thanks to Swamy Ayyappa, whose blessings, discipline and light have guided every step of my journey. Whatever clarity or strength this book carries is born from His grace.

To my parents, Leela Nair and VNB Nair, thank you for your endless love, your sacrifices, and the values you instilled in me. Your presence in my life is my greatest blessing, and your support gave me the courage to complete this work.

To my family members, including but not limited to Asha, Ayush, Manju, Kishore and Srida, thank you for bearing with me, for your encouragement, and for standing beside me through every phase of this journey.

To my friends and well-wishers, including but not limited to Satheesh, Vibu, Rada, Gopan and Manoj, who listened, encouraged and offered strength whenever I needed it, I am deeply grateful. Each of you has, in your own way, helped shape my spiritual journey, and for that I offer my sincere thanks.

I express my sincere appreciation to all my teachers and mentors, whose words, insights and example shaped many of the ideas shared in these pages. Your guidance continues to be a compass on my path.

I also wish to acknowledge the professional support that helped bring this book to its final form. My sincere thanks to Kausalya for editing and for all assistance in preparing this book for publication.

Finally, to the readers of this book, present and future, thank you for allowing these words into your life. May they serve you with humility, inspire your inner journey and strengthen your connection with your highest self.

May Swamy Ayyappa illumine your path, protect your steps and keep you forever in bliss.

With deep gratitude,
Vinod Nair